This Book
was Donated To

LRC Stoke Park

Date: 27/6/05

SELECTED POEMS

by

W. H. AUDEN

FABER AND FABER

24 Russell Square

London

First published in this edition 1968
by Faber and Faber Limited
24 Russell Square London WC1
Reprinted 1970
Printed in Great Britain by
R. MacLehose and Company Limited
The University Press Glasgow
All rights reserved
© this selection W. H. Auden
1968

ISBN 0 571 08521 0 (Faber Paper Covered Edition)

Contents

The Secret Agent

Control of the passes was, he saw, the key
To this new district, but who would get it?
He, the trained spy, had walked into the trap
For a bogus guide, seduced by the old tricks.

At Greenhearth was a fine site for a dam
And easy power, had they pushed the rail
Some stations nearer. They ignored his wires:
The bridges were unbuilt and trouble coming.

The street music seemed gracious now to one
For weeks up in the desert. Woken by water
Running away in the dark, he often had
Reproached the night for a companion
Dreamed of already. They would shoot, of course,
Parting easily two that were never joined.

The Watershed

Who stands, the crux left of the watershed,
On the wet road between the chafing grass
Below him sees dismantled washing-floors,
Snatches of tramline running to a wood,
An industry already comatose,
Yet sparsely living. A ramshackle engine
At Cashwell raises water; for ten years
It lay in flooded workings until this,
Its latter office, grudgingly performed.
And, further, here and there, though many dead
Lie under the poor soil, some acts are chosen
Taken from recent winters; two there were
Cleaned out a damaged shaft by hand, clutching
The winch a gale would tear them from; one died
During a storm, the fells impassable,
Not at his village, but in wooden shape
Through long abandoned levels nosed his way
And in his final valley went to ground.
Go home, now, stranger, proud of your young stock,
Stranger, turn back again, frustrate and vexed:
This land, cut off, will not communicate,
Be no accessory content to one
Aimless for faces rather there than here.
Beams from your car may cross a bedroom wall,
They wake no sleeper; you may hear the wind
Arriving driven from the ignorant sea
To hurt itself on pane, on bark of elm
Where sap unbaffled rises, being spring;
But seldom this. Near you, taller than grass,
Ears pose before decision, scenting danger.

O Where Are You Going

'O where are you going?' said reader to rider,
'That valley is fatal when furnaces burn,
Yonder's the midden whose odours will madden,
That gap is the grave where the tall return.'

'O do you imagine,' said fearer to farer,
'That dusk will delay on your path to the pass,
Your diligent looking discover the lacking
Your footsteps feel from granite to grass?'

'O what was that bird,' said horror to hearer,
'Did you see that shape in the twisted trees?
Behind you swiftly the figure comes softly,
The spot on your skin is a shocking disease.'

'Out of this house' — said rider to reader,
'Yours never will' — said farer to fearer,
'They're looking for you' — said hearer to horror,
As he left them there, as he left them there.

The Wanderer

Doom is dark and deeper than any sea-dingle.
Upon what man it fall
In spring, day-wishing flowers appearing,
Avalanche sliding, white snow from rock-face,
That he should leave his house,
No cloud-soft hand can hold him, restraint by women;
But ever that man goes
Through place-keepers, through forest trees,
A stranger to strangers over undried sea,
Houses for fishes, suffocating water,
Or lonely on fell as chat,
By pot-holed becks
A bird stone-haunting, an unquiet bird.

There head falls forward, fatigued at evening,
And dreams of home,
Waving from window, spread of welcome,
Kissing of wife under single sheet;
But waking sees
Bird-flocks nameless to him, through doorway voices
Of new men making another love.

Save him from hostile capture,
From sudden tiger's leap at corner;
Protect his house,
His anxious house where days are counted
From thunderbolt protect,
From gradual ruin spreading like a stain;
Converting number from vague to certain,
Bring joy, bring day of his returning,
Lucky with day approaching, with leaning dawn.

Ode

Though aware of our rank and alert to obey orders,
Watching with binoculars the movement of the grass for an
    ambush,
The pistol cocked, the code-word committed to memory;
        The youngest drummer
Knows all the peace-time stories like the oldest soldier,
        Though frontier-conscious,

About the tall white gods who landed from their open boat,
Skilled in the working of copper, appointing our feast-days,
Before the islands were submerged, when the weather was calm,
        The maned lion common,
An open wishing-well in every garden;
        When love came easy.

Perfectly certain, all of us, but not from the records,
Not from the unshaven agent who returned to the camp:
The pillar dug from the desert recorded only
        The sack of a city,
The agent clutching his side collapsed at our feet,
        'Sorry! They got me!'

Yes, they were living here once but do not now,
Yes, they are living still but do not here;
Lying awake after Lights Out a recruit may speak up:
        'Who told you all this?'
The tent-talk pauses a little till a veteran answers
        'Go to sleep, Sonny!'

Turning over he closes his eyes, and then in a moment
Sees the sun at midnight bright over cornfield and pasture,
Our hope. . . . Someone jostles him, fumbling for boots,
        Time to change guard:
Boy, the quarrel was before your time, the aggressor
        No one you know.

Your childish moments of awareness were all of our world,
At five you sprang, already a tiger in the garden,
At night your mother taught you to pray for our Daddy
        Far away fighting,
One morning you fell off a horse and your brother mocked you:
        'Just like a girl!'

Now we're due to parade on the square in front of the Cathedral,
When the bishop has blessed us, to file in after the choirboys,
To stand with the wine-dark conquerors in the roped-off pews,
        Shout ourselves hoarse:
'They ran like hares; we have broken them up like firewood;
        They fought against God'.

While in a great rift in the limestone miles away
At the same hour they gather, tethering their horses beside them;
A scarecrow prophet from a boulder foresees our judgment,
        Their oppressors howling;
And the bitter psalm is caught by the gale from the rocks:
        'How long shall they flourish?'

What have we all been doing to have made from Fear
That laconic war-bitten captain addressing them now?
Heart and head shall be keener, mood the more
        As our might lessens:
To have caused their shout 'We will fight till we lie down beside
        The Lord we have loved'.

There's Wrath who has learnt every trick of guerrilla warfare
The shamming dead, the night-raid, the feinted retreat;
Envy their brilliant pamphleteer, to lying
        As husband true,
Expert impersonator and linguist, proud of his power
        To hoodwink sentries.

Gluttony living alone, austerer than us,
Big simple Greed, Acedia famed with them all
For her stamina, keeping the outposts, and somewhere Lust,
        That skilful sapper,
Muttering to his fuses in a tunnel 'Could I meet here with Love,
        I would hug her to death'.

There are faces there for which for a very long time
We've been on the look-out, though often at home we imagined
Catching sight of a back or hearing a voice through a doorway
        We had found them at last;
Put our arms round their necks and looked in their eyes
    and discovered
        We were unlucky.

And some of them, surely, we seem to have seen before:
Why, that girl who rode off on her bicycle one fine
        summer evening
And never returned, she's there; and the banker we'd noticed
        Worried for weeks;
Till he failed to arrive one morning and his room was empty,
        Gone with a suitcase.

They speak of things done on the frontier we were never told,
The hidden path to their squat Pictish tower
They will never reveal though kept without sleep, for their
    code is
        'Death to the squealer':
They are brave, yes, though our newspapers mention
    their bravery
        In inverted commas.

But careful; back to our lines; it is unsafe there,
Passports are issued no longer; that area is closed;
There's no fire in the waiting-room now at the climbers'
    Junction,
            And all this year
Work has been stopped on the power-house; the wind
    whistles under
        The half-built culverts.

All leave is cancelled to-night; we must say good-bye.
We entrain at once for the North; we shall see in the morning
The headlands we're doomed to attack; snow down to
    the tide-line:
        Though the bunting signals
'Indoors before it's too late; cut peat for your fires,'
        We shall lie out there.

Legend

Enter with him
These legends, Love;
For him assume
Each diverse form,
To legend native,
As legend queer;
That he may do
What these require,
Be, Love, like him
To legend true.

When he to ease
His heart's disease
Must cross in sorrow
Corrosive seas,
As dolphin go;
As cunning fox
Guide through the rocks,
Tell in his ear
The common phrase
Required to please
The guardians there;
And when across
The livid marsh
Big birds pursue,
Again be true,
Between his thighs
As pony rise,
And swift as wind
Bear him away
Till cries and they
Are left behind.

But when at last,
These dangers passed,
His grown desire
Of legend tire,
Then, Love, standing
At legend's ending,
Claim your reward;
Submit your neck
To the ungrateful stroke
Of his reluctant sword,
That, starting back,
His eyes may look
Amazed on you,
Find what he wanted
Is faithful too
But disenchanted,
Love as love.

O What Is that Sound

O what is that sound which so thrills the ear
  Down in the valley drumming, drumming?
Only the scarlet soldiers, dear,
  The soldiers coming.

O what is that light I see flashing so clear
  Over the distance brightly, brightly?
Only the sun on their weapons, dear,
  As they step lightly.

O what are they doing with all that gear,
  What are they doing this morning, this morning?
Only their usual manoeuvres, dear,
  Or perhaps a warning.

O why have they left the road down there,
  Why are they suddenly wheeling, wheeling?
Perhaps a change in their orders, dear.
  Why are you kneeling?

O haven't they stopped for the doctor's care,
  Haven't they reined their horses, their horses?
Why, they are none of them wounded, dear,
  None of these forces.

O is it the parson they want, with white hair,
  Is it the parson, is it, is it?
No, they are passing his gateway, dear,
  Without a visit.

O it must be the farmer who lives so near.
  It must be the farmer so cunning, so cunning?
They have passed the farmyard already, dear,
  And now they are running.

O where are you going? Stay with me here!
  Were the vows you swore deceiving, deceiving?
No, I promised to love you, dear,
  But I must be leaving.

O it's broken the lock and splintered the door,
  O it's the gate where they're turning, turning;
Their boots are heavy on the floor
  And their eyes are burning.

As I walked out one Evening

As I walked out one evening
  Walking down Bristol Street,
The crowds upon the pavement
  Were fields of harvest wheat.

And down by the brimming river
  I heard a lover sing
Under an arch of the railway:
  'Love has no ending.

'I'll love you, dear, I'll love you
  Till China and Africa meet,
And the river jumps over the mountain
  And the salmon sing in the street,

'I'll love you till the ocean
  Is folded and hung up to dry
And the seven stars go squawking
  Like geese about the sky.

The years shall run like rabbits,
  For in my arms I hold
The Flower of the Ages,
  And the first love of the world.'

But all the clocks in the city
  Began to whirr and chime:
'O let not Time deceive you,
  You cannot conquer Time.

'In the burrows of the Nightmare
  Where Justice naked is,
Time watches from the shadow
  And coughs when you would kiss.

'In headaches and in worry
    Vaguely life leaks away,
And Time will have his fancy
    To-morrow or to-day.

'Into many a green valley
    Drifts the appalling snow;
Time breaks the threaded dances
    And the diver's brilliant bow.

'O plunge your hands in water,
    Plunge them in up to the wrist;
Stare, stare in the basin
    And wonder what you've missed.

'The glacier knocks in the cupboard,
    The desert sighs in the bed,
And the crack in the tea-cup opens
    A lane to the land of the dead.

'Where the beggars raffle the banknotes
    And the Giant is enchanting to Jack,
And the Lily-white Boy is a Roarer,
    And Jill goes down on her back.

'O look, look in the mirror,
    O look in your distress;
Life remains a blessing
    Although you cannot bless.

'O stand, stand at the window
    As the tears scald and start;
You shall love your crooked neighbour
    With your crooked heart.'

It was late, late in the evening,
    The lovers they were gone;
The clocks had ceased their chiming,
    And the deep river ran on.

Song of the Beggars

— 'O for doors to be open and an invite with gilded edges
To dine with Lord Lobcock and Count Asthma on the
    platinum benches,
With somersaults and fireworks, the roast and the smacking
    kisses' —
        Cried the cripples to the silent statue,
        The six beggared cripples.

— 'And Garbo's and Cleopatra's wits to go astraying,
In a feather ocean with me to go fishing and playing,
Still jolly when the cock has burst himself with crowing' —
        Cried the cripples to the silent statue,
        The six beggared cripples.

— 'And to stand on green turf among the craning yellow faces
Dependent on the chestnut, the sable, and Arabian horses,
And me with a magic crystal to foresee their places' —
        Cried the cripples to the silent statue.
        The six beggared cripples.

— 'And this square to be a deck and these pigeons canvas to rig,
And to follow the delicious breeze like a tantony pig
To the shaded feverless islands where the melons are big' —
        Cried the cripples to the silent statue,
        The six beggared cripples.

— 'And these shops to be turned to tulips in a garden bed,
And me with my crutch to thrash each merchant dead
As he pokes from a flower his bald and wicked head' —
        Cried the cripples to the silent statue,
        The six beggared cripples.

— 'And a hole in the bottom of heaven, and Peter and Paul
And each smug surprised saint like parachutes to fall,
And every one-legged beggar to have no legs at all' —
        Cried the cripples to the silent statue,
        The six beggared cripples.

Autumn Song

Now the leaves are falling fast,
Nurse's flowers will not last,
Nurses to their graves are gone,
But the prams go rolling on.

Whispering neighbours left and right
Daunt us from our true delight,
Able hands are forced to freeze
Derelict on lonely knees.

Close behind us on our track,
Dead in hundreds cry Alack,
Arms raised stiffly to reprove
In false attitudes of love.

Scrawny through a plundered wood,
Trolls run scolding for their food,
Owl and nightingale are dumb,
And the angel will not come.

Clear, unscaleable, ahead
Rise the Mountains of Instead,
From whose cold cascading streams
None may drink except in dreams.

Roman Wall Blues

Over the heather the wet wind blows,
I've lice in my tunic and a cold in my nose.

The rain comes pattering out of the sky,
I'm a Wall soldier, I don't know why.

The mist creeps over the hard grey stone,
My girl's in Tungria; I sleep alone.

Aulus goes hanging around her place,
I don't like his manners, I don't like his face.

Piso's a Christian, he worships a fish;
There'd be no kissing if he had his wish.

She gave me a ring but I diced it away;
I want my girl and I want my pay.

When I'm a veteran with only one eye
I shall do nothing but look at the sky.

Lullaby

Lay your sleeping head, my love,
Human on my faithless arm;
Time and fevers burn away
Individual beauty from
Thoughtful children, and the grave
Proves the child ephemeral:
But in my arms till break of day
Let the living creature lie,
Mortal, guilty, but to me
The entirely beautiful.

Soul and body have no bounds:
To lovers as they lie upon
Her tolerant enchanted slope
In their ordinary swoon,
Grave the vision Venus sends
Of supernatural sympathy,
Universal love and hope;
While an abstract insight wakes
Among the glaciers and the rocks
The hermit's carnal ecstasy.

Certainty, fidelity
On the stroke of midnight pass
Like vibrations of a bell
And fashionable madmen raise
Their pedantic boring cry:
Every farthing of the cost,
All the dreaded cards foretell,
Shall be paid, but from this night
Not a whisper, not a thought,
Not a kiss nor look be lost.

Beauty, midnight, vision dies:
Let the winds of dawn that blow
Softly round your dreaming head
Such a day of welcome show
Eye and knocking heart may bless,
Find our mortal world enough;
Noons of dryness find you fed
By the involuntary powers,
Nights of insult let you pass
Watched by every human love.

As He Is

Wrapped in a yielding air, beside
    The flower's noiseless hunger,
Close to the tree's clandestine tide,
    Close to the bird's high fever,
    Loud in his hope and anger,
Erect about a skeleton,
    Stands the expressive lover,
    Stands the deliberate man.

Beneath the hot unasking sun,
    Past stronger beasts and fairer
He picks his way, a living gun,
    With gun and lens and Bible,
    A militant enquirer,
The friend, the rash, the enemy,
    The essayist, the able,
    Able at times to cry.

The friendless and unhated stone
    Lies everywhere about him,
The Brothered-One, the Not-Alone,
    The brothered and the hated
    Whose family have taught him
To set against the large and dumb,
    The timeless and the rooted,
    His money and his time.

For mother's fading hopes become
    Dull wives to his dull spirits,
Soon dulled by nurse's moral thumb,
    That dullard fond betrayer,
    And, childish, he inherits,
So soon by legal father tricked,
    The tall imposing tower,
    Imposing, yes, but locked.

And ruled by dead men never met,
  By pious guess deluded,
Upon the stool of mania set
  Or stool of desolation,
  Sits murderous and clear-headed;
Enormous beauties round him move,
  For grandiose is his vision
  And grandiose his love.

Determined on Time's truthful shield
  The lamb must face the tigress,
Their faithful quarrel never healed
  Though, faithless, he consider
  His dream of vaguer ages,
Hunter and victim reconciled,
  The lion and the adder,
  The adder and the child.

Fresh loves betray him, every day
  Over his green horizon
A fresh deserter rides away,
  And miles away birds mutter
  Of ambush and of treason;
To fresh defeats he still must move,
  To further griefs and greater,
  And the defeat of grief.

Musée des Beaux Arts

About suffering they were never wrong,
The Old Masters : how well they understood
Its human position ; how it takes place
While someone else is eating or opening a window or just walking
    dully along ;
How, when the aged are reverently, passionately waiting
For the miraculous birth, there always must be
Children who did not specially want it to happen, skating
On a pond at the edge of the wood :

They never forgot
That even the dreadful martyrdom must run its course
Anyhow in a corner, some untidy spot
Where the dogs go on with their doggy life and the torturer's horse
Scratches its innocent behind on a tree.

In Brueghel's *Icarus*, for instance : how everything turns away
Quite leisurely from the disaster ; the ploughman may
Have heard the splash, the forsaken cry,
But for him it was not an important failure ; the sun shone
As it had to on the white legs disappearing into the green
Water ; and the expensive delicate ship that must have seen
Something amazing, a boy falling out of the sky,
Had somewhere to get to and sailed calmly on.

Sonnets from China

I

So from the years their gifts were showered: each
Grabbed at the one it needed to survive;
Bee took the politics that suit a hive,
Trout finned as trout, peach moulded into peach,

And were successful at their first endeavour.
The hour of birth their only time in college,
They were content with their precocious knowledge,
To know their station and be right for ever.

Till, finally, there came a childish creature
On whom the years could model any feature,
Fake, as chance fell, a leopard or a dove,

Who by the gentlest wind was rudely shaken,
Who looked for truth but always was mistaken,
And envied his few friends, and chose his love.

II

They wondered why the fruit had been forbidden:
It taught them nothing new. They hid their pride,
But did not listen much when they were chidden:
They knew exactly what to do outside.

They left. Immediately the memory faded
Of all they'd known: they could not understand
The dogs now who before had always aided;
The stream was dumb with whom they'd always planned.

They wept and quarrelled: freedom was so wild.
In front maturity as he ascended
Retired like a horizon from the child,

The dangers and the punishments grew greater,
And the way back by angels was defended
Against the poet and the legislator.

Only a smell had feelings to make known,
Only an eye could point in a direction,
The fountain's utterance was itself alone:
He, though, by naming thought to make connection

Between himself as hunter and his food;
He felt the interest in his throat and found
That he could send a servant to chop wood
Or kiss a girl to rapture with a sound.

They bred like locusts till they hid the green
And edges of the world: confused and abject,
A creature to his own creation subject,

He shook with hate for things he'd never seen,
Pined for a love abstracted from its object,
And was oppressed as he had never been.

He stayed, and was imprisoned in possession:
By turns the seasons guarded his one way,
The mountains chose the mother of his children,
In lieu of conscience the sun ruled his day.

Beyond him, his young cousins in the city
Pursued their rapid and unnatural courses,
Believed in nothing but were easy-going,
Far less afraid of strangers than of horses.

He, though, changed little,
But took his colour from the earth,
And grew in likeness to his fowls and cattle.

The townsman thought him miserly and simple,
Unhappy poets took him for the truth,
And tyrants held him up as an example.

His care-free swagger was a fine invention:
Life was too slow, too regular, too grave.
With horse and sword he drew the girls' attention,
A conquering hero, bountiful and brave,

To whom teen-agers looked for liberation:
At his command they left behind their mothers,
Their wits were sharpened by the long migration,
His camp-fires taught them all the horde were brothers.

Till what he came to do was done: unwanted,
Grown seedy, paunchy, pouchy, disappointed,
He took to drink to screw his nerves to murder,

Or sat in offices and stole,
Boomed at his children about Law and Order,
And hated life with heart and soul.

He watched the stars and noted birds in flight;
A river flooded or a fortress fell:
He made predictions that were sometimes right;
His lucky guesses were rewarded well.

Falling in love with Truth before he knew Her,
He rode into imaginary lands,
By solitude and fasting hoped to woo Her,
And mocked at those who served Her with their hands.

Drawn as he was to magic and obliqueness,
In Her he honestly believed, and when
At last She beckoned to him he obeyed,

Looked in Her eyes: awe-struck but unafraid,
Saw there reflected every human weakness,
And knew himself as one of many men.

VII

He was their servant (some say he was blind),
Who moved among their faces and their things:
Their feeling gathered in him like a wind
And sang. They cried 'It is a God that sings',

And honoured him, a person set apart,
Till he grew vain, mistook for personal song
The petty tremors of his mind or heart
At each domestic wrong.

Lines came to him no more; he had to make them
(With what precision was each strophe planned):
Hugging his gloom as peasants hug their land,

He stalked like an assassin through the town,
And glared at men because he did not like them,
But trembled if one passed him with a frown.

VIII

He turned his field into a meeting-place,
Evolved a tolerant ironic eye,
Put on a mobile money-changer's face,
Took up the doctrine of Equality.

Strangers were hailed as brothers by his clocks,
With roof and spire he built a human sky,
Stored random facts in a museum box,
To watch his treasure set a paper spy.

All grew so fast his life was overgrown,
Till he forgot what all had once been made for:
He gathered into crowds but was alone,

And lived expensively but did without,
No more could touch the earth which he had paid for,
Nor feel the love which he knew all about.

He looked in all His wisdom from His throne
Down on the humble boy who herded sheep,
And sent a dove. The dove returned alone:
Song put a charmed rusticity to sleep.

But He had planned such future for this youth:
Surely, His duty now was to compel,
To count on time to bring true love of truth
And, with it, gratitude. His eagle fell.

It did not work: His conversation bored
The boy, who yawned and whistled and made faces,
And wriggled free from fatherly embraces,

But with His messenger was always willing
To go where it suggested, and adored,
And learned from it so many ways of killing.

X

So an age ended, and its last deliverer died
In bed, grown idle and unhappy; they were safe:
The sudden shadow of a giant's enormous calf
Would fall no more at dusk across their lawns outside.

They slept in peace: in marshes here and there no doubt
A sterile dragon lingered to a natural death,
But in a year the slot had vanished from the heath;
A kobold's knocking in the mountain petered out.

Only the sculptors and the poets were half-sad,
And the pert retinue from the magician's house
Grumbled and went elsewhere. The vanquished powers
        were glad

To be invisible and free; without remorse
Struck down the silly sons who strayed into their course,
And ravished the daughters, and drove the fathers mad.

Certainly praise: let song mount again and again
For life as it blossoms out in a jar or a face,
For vegetal patience, for animal courage and grace:
Some have been happy; some, even, were great men.

But hear the morning's injured weeping and know why:
Ramparts and souls have fallen; the will of the unjust
Has never lacked an engine; still all princes must
Employ the fairly-noble unifying lie.

History opposes its grief to our buoyant song,
To our hope its warning. One star has warmed to birth
One puzzled species that has yet to prove its worth:

The quick new West is false, and prodigious but wrong
The flower-like Hundred Families who for so long
In the Eighteen Provinces have modified the earth.

Here war is harmless like a monument:
A telephone is talking to a man;
Flags on a map declare that troops were sent;
A boy brings milk in bowls. There is a plan

For living men in terror of their lives,
Who thirst at nine who were to thirst at noon,
Who can be lost and are, who miss their wives
And, unlike an idea, can die too soon.

Yet ideas can be true, although men die:
For we have seen a myriad faces
Ecstatic from one lie,

And maps can really point to places
Where life is evil now.
Nanking. Dachau.

Far from a cultural centre he was used:
Abandoned by his general and his lice,
Under a padded quilt he turned to ice
And vanished. He will never be perused

When this campaign is tidied into books:
No vital knowledge perished in that skull;
His jokes were stale; like wartime, he was dull;
His name is lost for ever like his looks.

Though runeless, to instructions from headquarters
He added meaning like a comma when
He joined the dust of China, that our daughters

Might keep their upright carriage, not again
Be shamed before the dogs, that, where are waters,
Mountains and houses, may be also men.

They are and suffer; that is all they do:
A bandage hides the place where each is living,
His knowledge of the world restricted to
A treatment metal instruments are giving.

They lie apart like epochs from each other
(Truth in their sense is how much they can bear;
It is not talk like ours but groans they smother),
From us remote as plants: we stand elsewhere.

For who when healthy can become a foot?
Even a scratch we can't recall when cured,
But are boisterous in a moment and believe

Reality is never injured, cannot
Imagine isolation: joy can be shared,
And anger, and the idea of love.

As evening fell the day's oppression lifted;
Tall peaks came into focus; it had rained:
Across wide lawns and cultured flowers drifted
The conversation of the highly trained.

Thin gardeners watched them pass and priced their shoes;
A chauffeur waited, reading in the drive,
For them to finish their exchange of views:
It looked a picture of the way to live.

Far off, no matter what good they intended,
Two armies waited for a verbal error
With well-made implements for causing pain,

And on the issue of their charm depended
A land laid waste with all its young men slain,
Its women weeping, and its towns in terror.

Our global story is not yet completed,
Crime, daring, commerce, chatter will go on,
But, as narrators find their memory gone,
Homeless, disterred, these know themselves defeated.

Some could not liken or change the young and mourn for
Some wounded myth that once made children good,
Some lost a world they never understood,
Some saw too clearly all that man was born for.

Loss is their shadow-wife, Anxiety
Receives them like a grand hotel, but where
They may regret they must: their doom to bear

Love for some far forbidden country, see
A native disapprove them with a stare
And Freedom's back in every door and tree.

Simple like all dream-wishes, they employ
The elementary rhythms of the heart,
Speak to our muscles of a need for joy:
The dying and the lovers bound to part

Hear them and have to whistle. Ever new,
They mirror every change in our position,
They are our evidence of how we do,
The very echoes of our lost condition.

Think in this year what pleased the dancers best,
When Austria died, when China was forsaken,
Shanghai in flames and Teruel re-taken.

France put her case before the world: *Partout
Il y a de la joie*. America addressed
Mankind: *Do you love me as I love you?*

Chilled by the Present, its gloom and its noise,
On waking we sigh for an ancient South,
A warm nude age of instinctive poise,
A taste of joy in an innocent mouth.

At night in our huts we dream of a part
In the balls of the Future: each ritual maze
Has a musical plan, and a musical heart
Can faultlessly follow its faultless ways.

We envy streams and houses that are sure,
But, doubtful, articled to error, we
Were never nude and calm as a great door,

And never will be faultless like our fountains:
We live in freedom by necessity,
A mountain people dwelling among mountains.

When all our apparatus of report
Confirms the triumph of our enemies,
Our frontier crossed, our forces in retreat,
Violence pandemic like a new disease,

And Wrong a charmer everywhere invited,
When Generosity gets nothing done,
Let us remember those who looked deserted:
To-night in China let me think of one

Who for ten years of drought and silence waited,
Until in Muzot all his being spoke,
And everything was given once for all.

Awed, grateful, tired, content to die, completed,
He went out in the winter night to stroke
That tower as one pets an animal.

Who needs their names? Another genus built
Those dictatorial avenues and squares,
Gigantic terraces, imposing stairs,
Men of a sorry kennel, racked by guilt,

Who wanted to persist in stone for ever:
Unloved, they had to leave material traces,
But these desired no status but our faces,
To dwell there incognito, glad we never

Can dwell on what they suffered, loved or were.
Earth grew them as a bay grows fishermen
Or hills a shepherd. While they breathed, the air

All breath took on a virtue; in our blood,
If we allow them, they can breathe again:
Happy their wish and mild to flower and flood.

(To E. M. Forster)

Though Italy and King's are far away,
And Truth a subject only bombs discuss,
Our ears unfriendly, still you speak to us,
Insisting that the inner life can pay.

As we dash down the slope of hate with gladness,
You trip us up like an unnoticed stone,
And, just when we are closeted with madness,
You interrupt us like the telephone.

Yes, we are Lucy, Turton, Philip: we
Wish international evil, are delighted
To join the jolly ranks of the benighted

Where reason is denied and love ignored,
But, as we swear our lie, Miss Avery
Comes out into the garden with a sword.

In Memory of W. B. Yeats

(d. Jan. 1939)

I

He disappeared in the dead of winter:
The brooks were frozen, the airports almost deserted,
And snow disfigured the public statues;
The mercury sank in the mouth of the dying day.
What instruments we have agree
The day of his death was a dark cold day.

Far from his illness
The wolves ran on through the evergreen forests,
The peasant river was untempted by the fashionable quays;
By mourning tongues
The death of the poet was kept from his poems.

But for him it was his last afternoon as himself,
An afternoon of nurses and rumours;
The provinces of his body revolted,
The squares of his mind were empty,
Silence invaded the suburbs,
The current of his feeling failed; he became his admirers.

Now he is scattered among a hundred cities
And wholly given over to unfamiliar affections,
To find his happiness in another kind of wood
And be punished under a foreign code of conscience.
The words of a dead man
Are modified in the guts of the living.

But in the importance and noise of to-morrow
When the brokers are roaring like beasts on the floor of the Bourse,
And the poor have the sufferings to which they are fairly
    accustomed,
And each in the cell of himself is almost convinced of his freedom,
A few thousand will think of this day
As one thinks of a day when one did something slightly unusual.
What instruments we have agree
The day of his death was a dark cold day.

II

You were silly like us; your gift survived it all:
The parish of rich women, physical decay,
Yourself. Mad Ireland hurt you into poetry.
Now Ireland has her madness and her weather still,
For poetry makes nothing happen: it survives
In the valley of its making where executives
Would never want to tamper, flows on south
From ranches of isolation and the busy griefs,
Raw towns that we believe and die in; it survives,
A way of happening, a mouth.

III

Earth, receive an honoured guest:
William Yeats is laid to rest.
Let the Irish vessel lie
Emptied of its poetry.

In the nightmare of the dark
All the dogs of Europe bark,
And the living nations wait,
Each sequestered in its hate;

Intellectual disgrace
Stares from every human face,
And the seas of pity lie
Locked and frozen in each eye.

Follow, poet, follow right
To the bottom of the night,
With your unconstraining voice
Still persuade us to rejoice;

With the farming of a verse
Make a vineyard of the curse,
Sing of human unsuccess
In a rapture of distress;

In the deserts of the heart
Let the healing fountain start,
In the prison of his days
Teach the free man how to praise.

Domesday Song

Jumbled in one common box
Of their dark stupidity,
Orchid, swan, and Caesar lie;
Time that tires of everyone
Has corroded all the locks
Thrown away the key for fun.

In its cleft the torrent mocks
Prophets who in days gone by
Made a profit on each cry,
Persona grata now with none;
And a jackass language shocks
Poets who can only pun.

Silence settles on the clocks;
Nursing mothers point a sly
Index finger at a sky,
Crimson in the setting sun;
In the valley of the fox
Gleams the barrel of a gun.

Once we could have made the docks,
Now it is too late to fly;
Once too often you and I
Did what we should not have done;
Round the rampant rugged rocks
Rude and ragged rascals run.

If I Could Tell You

Time will say nothing but I told you so,
Time only knows the price we have to pay;
If I could tell you I would let you know.

If we should weep when clowns put on their show,
If we should stumble when musicians play,
Time will say nothing but I told you so.

There are no fortunes to be told, although,
Because I love you more than I can say,
If I could tell you I would let you know.

The winds must come from somewhere when they blow,
There must be reasons why the leaves decay;
Time will say nothing but I told you so.

Perhaps the roses really want to grow,
The vision seriously intends to stay;
If I could tell you I would let you know.

Suppose the lions all get up and go,
And all the brooks and soldiers run away;
Will Time say nothing but I told you so?
If I could tell you I would let you know.

Atlantis

Being set on the idea
    Of getting to Atlantis,
You have discovered of course
    Only the Ship of Fools is
Making the voyage this year,
As gales of abnormal force
    Are predicted, and that you
    Must therefore be ready to
Behave absurdly enough
    To pass for one of The Boys,
At least appearing to love
    Hard liquor, horseplay and noise.

Should storms, as may well happen,
    Drive you to anchor a week
In some old harbour-city
    Of Ionia, then speak
With her witty scholars, men
Who have proved there cannot be
    Such a place as Atlantis:
    Learn their logic, but notice
How their subtlety betrays
    A simple enormous grief;
Thus they shall teach you the ways
    To doubt that you may believe.

If, later, you run aground
    Among the headlands of Thrace
Where with torches all night long
    A naked barbaric race
Leaps frenziedly to the sound
Of conch and dissonant gong;
    On that stony savage shore
    Strip off your clothes and dance, for
Unless you are capable
    Of forgetting completely
About Atlantis, you will
    Never finish your journey.

Again, should you come to gay
    Carthage or Corinth, take part
In their endless gaiety;
    And if in some bar a tart,
As she strokes your hair, should say
'This is Atlantis, dearie,'
    Listen with attentiveness
    To her life-story: unless
You become acquainted now
    With each refuge that tries to
Counterfeit Atlantis, how
    Will you recognize the true?

Assuming you beach at last
    Near Atlantis, and begin
The terrible trek inland
    Through squalid woods and frozen
Tundras where all are soon lost;
If, forsaken then, you stand,
    Dismissal everywhere,
    Stone and snow, silence and air,
Remember the noble dead
    And honour the fate you are,
Travelling and tormented,
    Dialectic and bizarre.

Stagger onward rejoicing;
    And even then if, perhaps
Having actually got
    To the last col, you collapse
With all Atlantis gleaming
Below you yet you cannot
    Descend, you should still be proud
Just to peep at Atlantis
    In a poetic vision:
Give thanks and lie down in peace,
    Having seen your salvation.

All the little household gods
    Have started crying, but say
Good-bye now, and put to sea.
    Farewell, dear friend, farewell: may
Hermes, master of the roads
And the four dwarf Kabiri,
    Protect and serve you always;
    And may the Ancient of Days
Provide for all you must do
    His invisible guidance,
Lifting up, friend, upon you
    The light of His countenance.

The Fall of Rome
(for Cyril Connolly)

The piers are pummelled by the waves;
In a lonely field the rain
Lashes an abandoned train;
Outlaws fill the mountain caves.

Fantastic grow the evening gowns;
Agents of the Fisc pursue
Absconding tax-defaulters through
The sewers of provincial towns.

Private rites of magic send
The temple prostitutes to sleep;
All the literati keep
An imaginary friend.

Cerebrotonic Cato may
Extol the Ancient Disciplines,
But the muscle-bound Marines
Mutiny for food and pay.

Caesar's double-bed is warm
As an unimportant clerk
Writes *I DO NOT LIKE MY WORK*
On a pink official form.

Unendowed with wealth or pity,
Little birds with scarlet legs,
Sitting on their speckled eggs,
Eye each flu-infected city.

Altogether elsewhere, vast
Herds of reindeer move across
Miles and miles of golden moss,
Silently and very fast.

A Walk After Dark

A cloudless night like this
Can set the spirit soaring:
After a tiring day
The clockwork spectacle is
Impressive in a slightly boring
Eighteenth-century way.

It soothed adolescence a lot
To meet so shameless a stare;
The things I did could not
Be so shocking as they said
If that would still be there
After the shocked were dead.

Now, unready to die
But already at the stage
When one starts to resent the young,
I am glad those points in the sky
May also be counted among
The creatures of middle-age.

It's cosier thinking of night
As more an Old People's Home
Than a shed for a faultless machine,
That the red pre-Cambrian light
Is gone like Imperial Rome
Or myself at seventeen.

Yet however much we may like
The stoic manner in which
The classical authors wrote,
Only the young and the rich
Have the nerve or the figure to strike
The lacrimae rerum note.

For the present stalks abroad
Like the past and its wronged again
Whimper and are ignored,
And the truth cannot be hid;
Somebody chose their pain,
What needn't have happened did.

Occurring this very night
By no established rule,
Some event may already have hurled
Its first little No at the right
Of the laws we accept to school
Our post-diluvian world:

But the stars burn on overhead,
Unconscious of final ends,
As I walk home to bed,
Asking what judgment waits
My person, all my friends,
And these United States.

The Quest

I

Out of it steps our future, through this door
Enigmas, executioners and rules,
Her Majesty in a bad temper or
A red-nosed Fool who makes a fool of fools.

Great persons eye it in the twilight for
A past it might so carelessly let in,
A widow with a missionary grin,
The foaming inundation at a roar.

We pile our all against it when afraid,
And beat upon its panels when we die:
By happening to be open once, it made

Enormous Alice see a wonderland
That waited for her in the sunshine and,
Simply by being tiny, made her cry.

II

All had been ordered weeks before the start
From the best firms at such work, instruments
To take the measure of all queer events,
And drugs to move the bowels or the heart.

A watch, of course, to watch impatience fly,
Lamps for the dark and shades against the sun;
Foreboding, too, insisted on a gun,
And coloured beads to soothe a savage eye.

In theory they were sound on Expectation,
Had there been situations to be in;
Unluckily they were their situation:

One should not give a poisoner medicine,
A conjurer fine apparatus, nor
A rifle to a melancholic bore.

III

Two friends who met here and embraced are gone,
Each to his own mistake; one flashes on
To fame and ruin in a rowdy lie,
A village torpor holds the other one,
Some local wrong where it takes time to die:
This empty junction glitters in the sun.

So at all quays and crossroads: who can tell
These places of decision and farewell
To what dishonour all adventure leads,
What parting gift could give that friend protection,
So orientated his vocation needs
The Bad Lands and the sinister directions?

All landscapes and all weathers freeze with fear,
But none have ever thought, the legends say,
The time allowed made it impossible;
For even the most pessimistic set
The limit of their errors at a year.
What friends could there be left then to betray,
What joy take longer to atone for; yet
Who would complete without the extra day
The journey that should take no time at all?

IV

No window in his suburb lights that bedroom where
A little fever heard large afternoons at play:
His meadows multiply; that mill, though, is not there
Which went on grinding at the back of love all day.

Nor all his weeping ways through weary wastes have found
The castle where his Greater Hallows are interned;
For broken bridges halt him, and dark thickets round
Some ruin where an evil heritage was burned.

Could he forget a child's ambition to be old
And institutions where it learned to wash and lie,
He'd tell the truth for which he thinks himself too young,

That everywhere on his horizon, all the sky,
Is now, as always, only waiting to be told
To be his father's house and speak his mother tongue.

V

In villages from which their childhoods came
Seeking Necessity, they had been taught
Necessity by nature is the same
No matter how or by whom it be sought.

The city, though, assumed no such belief,
But welcomed each as if he came alone,
The nature of Necessity like grief
Exactly corresponding to his own.

And offered them so many, every one
Found some temptation fit to govern him,
And settled down to master the whole craft

Of being nobody; sat in the sun
During the lunch-hour round the fountain rim,
And watched the country kids arrive and laughed.

VI

Ashamed to be the darling of his grief,
He joined a gang of rowdy stories where
His gift for magic quickly made him chief
Of all these boyish powers of the air;

Who turned his hungers into Roman food,
The town's asymmetry into a park;
All hours took taxis; any solitude
Became his flattered duchess in the dark.

But, if he wished for anything less grand,
The nights came padding after him like wild
Beasts that meant harm, and all the doors cried Thief;

And when Truth met him and put out her hand,
He clung in panic to his tall belief
And shrank away like an ill-treated child.

VII

His library annoyed him with its look
Of calm belief in being really there;
He threw away a rival's boring book,
And clattered panting up the spiral stair.

Swaying upon the parapet he cried:
'O Uncreated Nothing, set me free,
Now let Thy perfect be identified
Unending passion of the Night, with Thee.'

And his long-suffering flesh, that all the time
Had felt the simple cravings of the stone
And hoped to be rewarded for her climb,

Took it to be a promise when he spoke
That now at last she would be left alone,
And plunged into the college quad, and broke.

VIII

He watched with all his organs of concern
How princes walk, what wives and children say.
Re-opened old graves in his heart to learn
What laws the dead had died to disobey,

And came reluctantly to his conclusion:
'All the arm-chair philosophies are false;
To love another adds to the confusion;
The song of mercy is the Devil's Waltz.'

All that he put his hand to prospered so
That soon he was the very King of creatures,
Yet, in an autumn nightmare trembled, for,

Approaching down a ruined corridor,
Strode someone with his own distorted features
Who wept, and grew enormous, and cried Woe.

IX

This is an architecture for the odd;
Thus heaven was attacked by the afraid,
So once, unconsciously, a virgin made
Her maidenhead conspicuous to a god.

Here on dark nights while worlds of triumph sleep
Lost Love in abstract speculation burns,
And exiled Will to politics returns
In epic verse that makes its traitors weep.

Yet many come to wish their tower a well;
For those who dread to drown, of thirst may die,
Those who see all become invisible:

Here great magicians, caught in their own spell,
Long for a natural climate as they sigh
'Beware of Magic' to the passer-by.

X

They noticed that virginity was needed
To trap the unicorn in every case,
But not that, of those virgins who succeeded,
A high percentage had an ugly face.

The hero was as daring as they thought him,
But his peculiar boyhood missed them all;
The angel of a broken leg had taught him
The right precautions to avoid a fall.

So in presumption they set forth alone
On what, for them, was not compulsory,
And stuck half-way to settle in some cave
With desert lions to domesticity,

Or turned aside to be absurdly brave,
And met the ogre and were turned to stone.

His peasant parents killed themselves with toil
To let their darling leave a stingy soil
For any of those fine professions which
Encourage shallow breathing, and grow rich.

The pressure of their fond ambition made
Their shy and country-loving child afraid
No sensible career was good enough,
Only a hero could deserve such love.

So here he was without maps or supplies,
A hundred miles from any decent town;
The desert glared into his blood-shot eyes,
The silence roared displeasure:
                                        looking down,
He saw the shadow of an Average Man
Attempting the exceptional, and ran.

Incredulous, he stared at the amused
Official writing down his name among
Those whose request to suffer was refused.

The pen ceased scratching: though he came too late
To join the martyrs, there was still a place
Among the tempters for a caustic tongue

To test the resolution of the young
With tales of the small failings of the great,
And shame the eager with ironic praise.

Though mirrors might be hateful for a while,
Women and books would teach his middle age
The fencing wit of an informal style,
To keep the silences at bay and cage
His pacing manias in a worldly smile.

The over-logical fell for the witch
Whose argument converted him to stone,
Thieves rapidly absorbed the over-rich,
The over-popular went mad alone,
And kisses brutalized the over-male.

As agents their importance quickly ceased;
Yet, in proportion as they seemed to fail,
Their instrumental value was increased
For one predestined to attain their wish.

By standing stones the blind can feel their way,
Wild dogs compel the cowardly to fight,
Beggars assist the slow to travel light,
And even madmen manage to convey
Unwelcome truths in lonely gibberish.

Fresh addenda are published every day
To the encyclopedia of the Way,

Linguistic notes and scientific explanations,
And texts for schools with modernized spelling and illustrations.

Now everyone knows the hero must choose the old horse,
Abstain from liquor and sexual intercourse,

And look out for a stranded fish to be kind to:
Now everyone thinks he could find, had he a mind to,

The way through the waste to the chapel in the rock
For a vision of the Triple Rainbow or the Astral Clock,

Forgetting his information comes mostly from married men
Who liked fishing and a flutter on the horses now and then.

And how reliable can any truth be that is got
By observing oneself and then just inserting a Not?

Suppose he'd listened to the erudite committee,
He would have only found where not to look;
Suppose his terrier when he whistled had obeyed,
It would not have unearthed the buried city;
Suppose he had dismissed the careless maid,
The cryptogram would not have fluttered from the book.

'I was not I', he cried as, healthy and astounded,
He stepped across a predecessor's skull;
'A nonsense jingle simply came into my head
And left the intellectual Sphinx dumbfounded;
I won the Queen because my hair was red;
The terrible adventure is a little dull.'

Hence Failure's torment: 'Was I doomed in any case,
Or would I not have failed had I believed in Grace?'

He parried every question that they hurled:
'What did the Emperor tell you?' 'Not to push?'
'What is the greatest wonder of the world?'
'The bare man Nothing in the Beggar's Bush.'

Some muttered; 'He is cagey for effect.
A hero owes a duty to his fame.
He looks too like a grocer for respect.'
Soon they slipped back into his Christian name.

The only difference that could be seen
From those who'd never risked their lives at all
Was his delight in details and routine:

For he was always glad to mow the grass,
Pour liquids from large bottles into small,
Or look at clouds through bits of coloured glass.

Others had found it prudent to withdraw
Before official pressure was applied,
Embittered robbers outlawed by the Law,
Lepers in terror of the terrified.

But no one else accused these of a crime;
They did not look ill: old friends, overcome,
Stared as they rolled away from talk and time
Like marbles out into the blank and dumb.

The crowd clung all the closer to convention,
Sunshine and horses, for the sane know why
The even numbers should ignore the odd:

The Nameless is what no free people mention;
Successful men know better than to try
To see the face of their Absconded God.

Spinning upon their central thirst like tops,
They went the Negative Way towards the Dry;
By empty caves beneath an empty sky
They emptied out their memories like slops,

Which made a foul marsh as they dried to death,
Where monsters bred who forced them to forget
The lovelies their consent avoided; yet,
Still praising the Absurd with their last breath,

They seeded out into their miracles:
The images of each grotesque temptation
Became some painter's happiest inspiration,

And barren wives and burning virgins came
To drink the pure cold water of their wells,
And wish for beaux and children in their name.

Poet, oracle, and wit
Like unsuccessful anglers by
The ponds of apperception sit,
Baiting with the wrong request
The vectors of their interest,
At nightfall tell the angler's lie.

With time in tempest everywhere,
To rafts of frail assumption cling
The saintly and the insincere;
Enraged phenomena bear down
In overwhelming waves to drown
Both sufferer and suffering.

The waters long to hear our question put
Which would release their longed-for answer, but.

Within these gates all opening begins:
White shouts and flickers through its green and red.
Where children play at seven earnest sins
And dogs believe their tall conditions dead.

Her adolescence into number breaks
The perfect circle time can draw on stone,
And flesh forgives division as it makes
Another's moment of consent its own.

All journeys die here: wish and weight are lifted:
Where often round some old maid's desolation
Roses have flung their glory like a cloak,

The gaunt and great, the famed for conversation
Blushed in the stare of evening as they spoke
And felt their centre of volition shifted.

from *The Sea and the Mirror*

II

THE SUPPORTING CAST
SOTTO VOCE

ANTONIO

As all the pigs have turned back into men
And the sky is auspicious and the sea
Calm as a clock, we can all go home again.

Yes, it undoubtedly looks as if we
Could take life as easily now as tales
Write ever-after : not only are the

Two heads silhouetted against the sails
— And kissing, of course — well-built, but the lean
Fool is quite a person, the fingernails

Of the dear old butler for once quite clean,
And the royal passengers quite as good
As rustics, perhaps better, for they mean

What they say, without, as a rustic would,
Casting reflections on the courtly crew.
Yes, Brother Prospero, your grouping could

Not be more effective given a few
Incomplete objects and a nice warm day,
What a lot a little music can do.

Dotted about the deck they doze or play,
Your loyal subjects all, grateful enough
To know their place and believe what you say.

Antonio, sweet brother, has to laugh.
How easy you have made it to refuse
Peace to your greatness ! Break your wand in half,

The fragments will join; burn your books or lose
Them in the sea, they will soon reappear,
Not even damaged: as long as I choose

To wear my fashion, whatever you wear
Is a magic robe; while I stand outside
Your circle, the will to charm is still there.

As I exist so you shall be denied,
Forced to remain our melancholy mentor,
The grown-up man, the adult in his pride,

Never have time to curl up at the centre
Time turns on when completely reconciled,
Never become and therefore never enter
The green occluded pasture as a child.

> *Your all is partial, Prospero;*
> *My will is all my own:*
> *Your need to love shall never know*
> *Me: I am I, Antonio,*
> *By choice myself alone.*

FERDINAND

Flesh, fair, unique, and you, warm secret that my kiss
Follows into meaning Miranda, solitude
Where my omissions are, still possible, still good,
Dear Other at all times, retained as I do this,

From moment to moment as you enrich them so
Inherit me, my cause, as I would cause you now

With mine your sudden joy, two wonders as one vow
Pre-empting all, here, there, for ever, long ago.

I would smile at no other promise than touch, taste, sight,
Were there not, my enough, my exaltation, to bless
As world is offered world, as I hear it tonight

62

Pleading with ours for us, another tenderness
That neither without either could or would possess,
The Right Required Time, The Real Right Place, O Light.

> One bed is empty, Prospero,
>   My person is my own;
> Hot Ferdinand will never know
> The flame with which Antonio
>   Burns in the dark alone.

STEPHANO

Embrace me, belly, like a bride;
Dear daughter, for the weight you drew
From humble pie and swallowed pride,
Believe the boast in which you grew:
Where mind meets matter, both should woo;
Together let us learn that game
The high play better than the blue:
A lost thing looks for a lost name.

Behind your skirts your son must hide
When disappointments bark and boo;
Brush my heroic ghosts aside,
Wise nanny, with a vulgar pooh:
Exchanging cravings we pursue
Alternately a single aim:
Between the bottle and the 'loo'
A lost thing looks for a lost name.

Though in the long run satisfied,
The will of one by being two
At every moment is denied;
Exhausted glasses wonder who
Is self and sovereign, I or You?
We cannot both be what we claim,
The real Stephano — Which is true?
A lost thing looks for a lost name.

Child? Mother? Either grief will do;
The need for pardon is the same,
The contradiction is not new:
A lost thing looks for a lost name.
   One glass is untouched, Prospero,
      My nature is my own;
   Inert Stephano does not know
   The feast at which Antonio
      Toasts One and One alone.

GONZALO

Evening, grave, immense, and clear,
Overlooks our ship whose wake
Lingers undistorted on
Sea and silence; I look back
For the last time as the sun
Sets behind that island where
All our loves were altered: yes,
My prediction came to pass,
Yet I am not justified,
And I weep but not with pride.
Not in me the credit for
Words I uttered long ago
Whose glad meaning I betrayed;
Truths today admitted, owe
Nothing to the councillor
In whose booming eloquence
Honesty became untrue.
Am I not Gonzalo who
By his self-reflection made
Consolation an offence?

There was nothing to explain:
Had I trusted the Absurd
And straightforward note by note
Sung exactly what I heard,
Such immediate delight
Would have taken there and then
Our common welkin by surprise,
All would have begun to dance
Jigs of self-deliverance.
It was I prevented this,
Jealous of my native ear,
Mine the art which made the song
Sound ridiculous and wrong,
I whose interference broke
The gallop into jog-trot prose
And by speculation froze
Vision into an idea,
Irony into a joke,
Till I stood convicted of
Doubt and insufficient love.

Farewell, dear island of our wreck:
All have been restored to health,
All have seen the Commonwealth,
There is nothing to forgive.
Since a storm's decision gave
His subjective passion back
To a meditative man,
Even reminiscence can
Comfort ambient troubles like
Some ruined tower by the sea
Whence boyhoods growing and afraid
Learn a formula they need
In solving their mortality,

Even rusting flesh can be
A simple locus now, a bell
The Already There can lay
Hands on if at any time
It should feel inclined to say
To the lonely — 'Here I am,'
To the anxious — 'All is well.'

One tongue is silent, Prospero,
*   My language is my own;*
Decayed Gonzalo does not know
The shadow that Antonio
*   Talks to, at noon, alone.*

ADRIAN AND FRANCISCO

Good little sunbeams must learn to fly,
But it's madly ungay when the goldfish die.
*   One act is censored, Prospero,*
*   My audience is my own;*
*   Nor Adrian nor Francisco know*
*   The drama that Antonio*
*   Plays in his head alone.*

ALONSO

Dear Son, when the warm multitudes cry,
Ascend your throne majestically,
But keep in mind the waters where fish
See sceptres descending with no wish
To touch them; sit regal and erect,
But imagine the sand where a crown
Has the status of a broken-down
Sofa or mutilated statue:
Remember as bells and cannon boom
The cold deep that does not envy you.
The sunburnt superficial kingdom
Where a king is an object.

Expect no help from others, for who
Talk sense to princes or refer to
The scorpion in official speeches
As they unveil some granite Progress
Leading a child and holding a bunch
Of lilies? In their Royal Zoos the
Shark and the octopus are tactfully
Omitted; synchronized clocks march on
Within their powers: without, remain
The ocean flats where no subscription
Concerts are given, the desert plain
Where there is nothing for lunch.

Only your darkness can tell you what
A prince's ornate mirror dare not,
Which you should fear more — the sea in which
A tyrant sinks entangled in rich
Robes while a mistress turns a white back
Upon his splutter, or the desert
Where an emperor stands in his shirt
While his diary is read by sneering
Beggars, and far off he notices
A lean horror flapping and hopping
Toward him with inhuman swiftness:
Learn from your dreams what you lack,

For as your fears are, so must you hope.
The Way of Justice is a tightrope
Where no prince is safe for one instant
Unless he trust his embarrassment,
As in his left ear the siren sings
Meltingly of water and a night
Where all flesh had peace, and on his right
The efreet offers a brilliant void
Where his mind could be perfectly clear
And all his limitations destroyed:
Many young princes soon disappear
To join all the unjust kings.

So, if your prosper, suspect those bright
Mornings when you whistle with a light
Heart. You are loved; you have never seen
The harbour so still, the park so green,
So many well-fed pigeons upon
Cupolas and triumphal arches,
So many stags and slender ladies
Beside the canals. Remember when
Your climate seems a permanent home
For marvellous creatures and great men,
What griefs and convulsions startled Rome,
Ecbatana, Babylon.

How narrow the space, how slight the chance
For civil pattern and importance
Between the watery vagueness and
The triviality of the sand,
How soon the lively trip is over
From loose craving to sharp aversion,
Aimless jelly to paralyzed bone:
At the end of each successful day
Remember that the fire and the ice
Are never more than one step away
From the temperate city; it is
But a moment to either.

But should you fail to keep your kingdom
And, like your father before you, come
Where thought accuses and feeling mocks,
Believe your pain: praise the scorching rocks
For their desiccation of your lust,
Thank the bitter treatment of the tide
For its dissolution of your pride,
That the whirlwind may arrange your will
And the deluge release it to find
The spring in the desert, the fruitful
Island in the sea, where flesh and mind
Are delivered from mistrust.

68

Blue the sky beyond her humming sail
As I sit today by our ship's rail
Watching exuberant porpoises
Escort us homeward and writing this
For you to open when I am gone:
Read it, Ferdinand, with the blessing
Of Alonso, your father, once King
Of Naples, now ready to welcome
Death, but rejoicing in a new love,
A new peace, having heard the solemn
Music strike and seen the statue move
To forgive our illusion.

One crown is lacking, Prospero,
    My empire is my own;
Dying Alonso does not know
The diadem Antonio
    Wears in his world alone.

MASTER AND BOATSWAIN

At Dirty Dick's and Sloppy Joe's
    We drank our liquor straight,
Some went upstairs with Margery,
    And some, alas, with Kate;
And two by two like cat and mouse
The homeless played at keeping house.

There Wealthy Meg, the Sailor's Friend,
    And Marion, cow-eyed,
Opened their arms to me but I
    Refused to step inside;
I was not looking for a cage
In which to mope in my old age.

The nightingales are sobbing in
  The orchards of our mothers,
And hearts that we broke long ago
  Have long been breaking others;
Tears are round, the sea is deep:
Roll them overboard and sleep.

One gaze points elsewhere, Prospero,
  My compass is my own;
Nostalgic sailors do not know
The waters where Antonio
  Sails on and on alone.

SEBASTIAN

My rioters all disappear, my dream
Where Prudence flirted with a naked sword,
Securely vicious, crumbles; it is day;
Nothing has happened; we are all alive:
I am Sebastian, wicked still, my proof
Of mercy that I wake without a crown.

What sadness signalled to our children's day
Where each believed all wishes wear a crown
And anything pretended is alive,
That one by one we plunged into that dream
Of solitude and silence where no sword
Will ever play once it is called a proof?

The arrant jewel singing in his crown
Persuaded me my brother was a dream
I should not love because I had not proof,
Yet all my honesty assumed a sword;
To think his death I thought myself alive
And stalked infected through the blooming day.

The lie of Nothing is to promise proof
To any shadow that there is no day
Which cannot be extinguished with some sword,
To want and weakness that the ancient crown
Envies the childish head, murder a dream
Wrong only while its victim is alive.

O blessed be bleak Exposure on whose sword,
Caught unawares, we prick ourselves alive!
Shake Failure's bruising fist! Who else would crown
Abominable error with a proof?
I smile because I tremble, glad today
To be ashamed, not anxious, not a dream.

Children are playing, brothers are alive,
And not a heart or stomach asks for proof
That all this dearness is no lovers' dream;
Just Now is what it might be every day,
Right Here is absolute and needs no crown,
Ermine or trumpets, protocol or sword.

In dream all sins are easy, but by day
It is defeat gives proof we are alive:
The sword we suffer is the guarded crown.

> *One face cries nothing, Prospero,*
> *My conscience is my own;*
> *Pallid Sebastian does not know*
> *The dream in which Antonio*
> *Fights the white bull alone.*

TRINCULO

Mechanic, merchant, king,
Are warmed by the cold clown
Whose head is in the clouds
And never can get down.

Into a solitude
Undreamed of by their fat
Quick dreams have lifted me;
The north wind steals my hat.

On clear days I can see
Green acres far below,
And the red roof where I
Was Little Trinculo.

There lies that solid world
These hands can never reach;
My history, my love,
Is but a choice of speech.

A terror shakes my tree,
A flock of words fly out,
Whereat a laughter shakes
The busy and devout.

Wild images, come down
Out of your freezing sky,
That I, like shorter men,
May get my joke and die.

Our note is jarring, Prospero,
  My humour is my own;
Tense Trinculo will never know
The paradox Antonio
  Laughs at, in woods, alone.

MIRANDA

My Dear One is mine as mirrors are lonely,
As the poor and sad are real to the good king,
And the high green hill sits always by the sea.

Up jumped the Black Man behind the elder tree,
Turned a somersault and ran away waving;
My Dear One is mine as mirrors are lonely.

The Witch gave a squawk; her venomous body
Melted into light as water leaves a spring
And the high green hill sits always by the sea.

At his crossroads, too, the Ancient prayed for me;
Down his wasted cheeks tears of joy were running:
My Dear One is mine as mirrors are lonely.

He kissed me awake, and no one was sorry;
The sun shone on sails, eyes, pebbles, anything,
And the high green hill sits always by the sea.

So, to remember our changing garden, we
Are linked as children in a circle dancing:
My Dear One is mine as mirrors are lonely,
And the high green hill sits always by the sea.

> *One link is missing, Prospero,*
>   *My magic is my own;*
> *Happy Miranda does not know*
> *The figure that Antonio,*
> *The Only One, Creation's O*
>   *Dances for Death alone.*

In Praise of Limestone

If it form the one landscape that we, the inconstant ones,
  Are consistently homesick for, this is chiefly
Because it dissolves in water. Mark these rounded slopes
  With their surface fragrance of thyme and, beneath,
A secret system of caves and conduits; hear the springs
  That spurt out everywhere with a chuckle,
Each filling a private pool for its fish and carving
  Its own little ravine whose cliffs entertain
The butterfly and the lizard; examine this region
  Of short distances and definite places:
What could be more like Mother or a fitter background
  For her son, the flirtatious male who lounges
Against a rock in the sunlight, never doubting
  That for all his faults he is loved; whose works are but
Extensions of his power to charm? From weathered outcrop
  To hill-top temple, from appearing waters to
Conspicuous fountains, from a wild to a formal vineyard,
  Are ingenious but short steps that a child's wish
To receive more attention than his brothers, whether
  By pleasing or teasing, can easily take.

Watch, then, the band of rivals as they climb up and down
  Their steep stone gennels in twos and threes, at times
Arm in arm, but never, thank God, in step; or engaged
  On the shady side of a square at midday in
Voluble discourse, knowing each other too well to think
  There are any important secrets, unable
To conceive a god whose temper-tantrums are moral
  And not to be pacified by a clever line
Or a good lay: for, accustomed to a stone that responds,
  They have never had to veil their faces in awe
Of a crater whose blazing fury could not be fixed;
  Adjusted to the local needs of valleys
Where everything can be touched or reached by walking,
  Their eyes have never looked into infinite space

74

Through the lattice-work of a nomad's comb; born lucky,
    Their legs have never encountered the fungi
And insects of the jungle, the monstrous forms and lives
    With which we have nothing, we like to hope, in common.
So, when one of them goes to the bad, the way his mind works
    Remains comprehensible: to become a pimp
Or deal in fake jewellery or ruin a fine tenor voice
    For effects that bring down the house, could happen to all
But the best and the worst of us . . .

                      That is why, I suppose,
    The best and worst never stayed here long but sought
Immoderate soils where the beauty was not so external,
    The light less public and the meaning of life
Something more than a mad camp. 'Come!' cried the granite
    wastes,
    'How evasive is your humour, how accidental
Your kindest kiss, how permanent is death.' (Saints-to-be
    Slipped away sighing.) 'Come!' purred the clays and gravels.
'On our plains there is room for armies to drill; rivers
    Wait to be tamed and slaves to construct you a tomb
In the grand manner: soft as the earth is mankind and both
    Need to be altered.' (Intendant Caesars rose and
Left, slamming the door.) But the really reckless were fetched
    By an older colder voice, the oceanic whisper:
'I am the solitude that asks and promises nothing;
    That is how I shall set you free. There is no love;
There are only the various envies, all of them sad.'
    They were right, my dear, all those voices were right
And still are; this land is not the sweet home that it looks,
    Nor its peace the historical calm of a site
Where something was settled once and for all: A backward
    And dilapidated province, connected
To the big busy world by a tunnel, with a certain
    Seedy appeal, is that all it is now? Not quite:
It has a worldly duty which in spite of itself
    It does not neglect, but calls into question
All the Great Powers assume; it disturbs our rights. The poet,
    Admired for his earnest habit of calling

The sun the sun, his mind Puzzle, is made uneasy
  By these marble statues which so obviously doubt
His antimythological myth ; and these gamins,
  Pursuing the scientist down the tiled colonnade
With such lively offers, rebuke his concern for Nature's
  Remotest aspects : I, too, am reproached, for what
And how much you know. Not to lose time, not to get caught,
  Not to be left behind, not, please ! to resemble
The beasts who repeat themselves, or a thing like water
  Or stone whose conduct can be predicted, these
Are our Common Prayer, whose greatest comfort is music
  Which can be made anywhere, is invisible,
And does not smell. In so far as we have to look forward
  To death as a fact, no doubt we are right : But if
Sins can be forgiven, if bodies rise from the dead,
  These modifications of matter into
Innocent athletes and gesticulating fountains,
  Made solely for pleasure, make a further point :
The blessed will not care what angle they are regarded from,
  Having nothing to hide. Dear, I know nothing of
Either, but when I try to image a faultless love
  Or the life to come, what I hear is the murmur
Of underground streams, what I see is a limestone landscape.

Fleet Visit

The sailors come ashore
Out of their hollow ships,
Mild-looking middle class boys
Who read the comic strips;
One baseball game is more
To them than fifty Troys.

They look a bit lost, set down
In this unamerican place
Where natives pass with laws
And futures of their own;
They are not here because
But only just-in-case.

The whore and ne'er-do-well
Who pester them with junk
In their grubby ways at least
Are serving the Social Beast;
They neither make nor sell —
No wonder they get drunk.

But their ships on the vehement blue
Of this harbour actually gain
From having nothing to do;
Without a human will
To tell them whom to kill
Their structures are humane

And, far from looking lost,
Look as if they were meant
To be pure abstract design
By some master of pattern and line,
Certainly worth every cent
Of the billions they must have cost.

The Shield of Achilles

She looked over his shoulder
 For vines and olive trees,
Marble well-governed cities
 And ships upon untamed seas,
But there on the shining metal
 His hands had put instead
An artificial wilderness
 And a sky like lead.

A plain without a feature, bare and brown,
 No blade of grass, no sign of neighbourhood,
Nothing to eat and nowhere to sit down,
 Yet, congregated on its blankness, stood
 An unintelligible multitude,
A million eyes, a million boots in line,
Without expression, waiting for a sign.

Out of the air a voice without a face
 Proved by statistics that some cause was just
In tones as dry and level as the place:
 No one was cheered and nothing was discussed;
 Column by column in a cloud of dust
They marched away enduring a belief
Whose logic brought them, somewhere else, to grief.

She looked over his shoulder
 For ritual pieties,
White flower-garlanded heifers,
 Libation and sacrifice,
But there on the shining metal
 Where the altar should have been,
She saw by his flickering forge-light
 Quite another scene.

Barbed wire enclosed an arbitrary spot
    Where bored officials lounged (one cracked a joke)
And sentries sweated for the day was hot:
    A crowd of ordinary decent folk
    Watched from without and neither moved nor spoke
As three pale figures were led forth and bound
To three posts driven upright in the ground.

The mass and majesty of this world, all
    That carries weight and always weighs the same
Lay in the hands of others; they were small
    And could not hope for help and no help came:
    What their foes liked to do was done, their shame
Was all the worst could wish; they lost their pride
And died as men before their bodies died.

        She looked over his shoulder
           For athletes at their games,
        Men and women in a dance
           Moving their sweet limbs
        Quick, quick, to music,
           But there on the shining shield
        His hands had set no dancing-floor
           But a weed-choked field.

A ragged urchin, aimless and alone,
    Loitered about that vacancy, a bird
Flew up to safety from his well-aimed stone:
    That girls are raped, that two boys knife a third,
    Were axioms to him, who'd never heard
Of any world where promises were kept,
Or one could weep because another wept.

The thin-lipped armourer,
   Hephaestos hobbled away,
Thetis of the shining breasts
   Cried out in dismay
At what the god had wrought
   To please her son, the strong
Iron-hearted man-slaying Achilles
   Who would not live long.

The Sabbath

Waking on the Seventh Day of Creation,
    They cautiously sniffed the air:
The most fastidious nostril among them admitted
    That fellow was no longer there.

Herbivore, parasite, predator scouted,
    Migrants flew fast and far —
Not a trace of his presence: holes in the earth,
    Beaches covered with tar,

Ruins and metallic rubbish in plenty
    Were all that was left of him
Whose birth on the Sixth had made of that day
    An unnecessary interim.

Well, that fellow had never really smelled
    Like a creature who would survive:
No grace, address or faculty like those
    Born on the First Five.

Back, then, at last on a natural economy,
    Now His Impudence was gone,
Looking exactly like what it was,
    The Seventh Day went on,

Beautiful, happy, perfectly pointless. . . .
    A rifle's ringing crack
Split their Arcadia wide open, cut
    Their Sabbath nonsense short.

For whom did they think they had been created?
    That fellow was back,
More bloody-minded than they remembered,
    More god-like than they thought.

First Things First

Woken, I lay in the arms of my own warmth and listened
To a storm enjoying its storminess in the winter dark
Till my ear, as it can when half-asleep or half-sober,
Set to work to unscramble that interjectory uproar,
Construing its airy vowels and watery consonants
Into a love-speech indicative of a Proper Name.

Scarcely the tongue I should have chosen, yet, as well
As harshness and clumsiness would allow, it spoke in your praise,
Kenning you a god-child of the Moon and the West Wind
With power to tame both real and imaginary monsters,
Likening your poise of being to an upland county,
Here green on purpose, there pure blue for luck.

Loud though it was, alone as it certainly found me,
It reconstructed a day of peculiar silence
When a sneeze could be heard a mile off, and had me walking
On a headland of lava beside you, the occasion as ageless
As the stare of any rose, your presence exactly
So once, so valuable, so there, so now.

This, moreover, at an hour when only too often
A smirking devil annoys me in beautiful English,
Predicting a world where every sacred location
Is a sand-buried site all cultured Texans do,
Misinformed and thoroughly fleeced by their guides,
And gentle hearts are extinct like Hegelian Bishops.

Grateful, I slept till a morning that would not say
How much it believed of what I said the storm had said
But quietly drew my attention to what had been done
— So many cubic metres the more in my cistern
Against a leonine summer —, putting first things first:
Thousands have lived without love, not one without water.

The Old Man's Road

Across the Great Schism, through our whole landscape,
Ignoring God's Vicar and God's Ape,

Under their noses, unsuspected,
The Old Man's Road runs as it did

When a light subsoil, a simple ore
Were still in vogue : true to His wherefore,

By stiles, gates, hedge-gaps it goes
Over ploughland, woodland, cow meadows,

Past shrines to a cosmological myth
No heretic today would be caught dead with,

Near hill-top rings that were so safe then,
Now stormed easily by small children.

(Shepherds use bits in the high mountains,
Hamlets take stretches for Lovers' Lanes)

Then through cities threads its odd way,
Now without gutters, a Thieves' Alley,

Now with green lamp-posts and white curb,
The smart Crescent of a high-toned suburb,

Giving wide berth to an old Cathedral,
Running smack through a new Town Hall,

Unlookable for, by logic, by guess :
Yet some strike it, and are struck fearless.

No life can know it, but no life
That sticks to this course can be made captive,

And who wander with it are not stopped at
Borders by guards of some Theocrat,

Crossing the pass so almost where
His searchlight squints but no closer

(And no further where it might by chance):
So in summer sometimes, without hindrance,

Apotropaically scowling, a tinker
Shuffles past, in the waning year

Potters a coleopterist, poking
Through yellow leaves, and a youth in spring

Trots by after a new excitement,
His true self, hot on the scent.

The Old Man leaves his Road to those
Who love it no less since it lost purpose,

Who never ask what History is up to,
So cannot act as if they knew:

Assuming a freedom its Powers deny,
Denying its Powers, they pass freely.

Friday's Child

*In memory of Dietrcih Bonhoeffer, martyred
at Flossenburg, April 9th, 1945*

He told us we were free to choose
But, children as we were, we thought —
'Paternal Love will only use
   Force in the last resort

On those too bumptious to repent.' —
Accustomed to religious dread,
It never crossed our minds He meant
   Exactly what He said.

Perhaps He frowns, perhaps He grieves,
But it seems idle to discuss
If anger or compassion leaves
   The bigger bangs to us.

What reverence is rightly paid
To a Divinity so odd
He lets the Adam whom He made
   Perform the Acts of God?

It might be jolly if we felt
Awe at this Universal Man;
(When kings were local, people knelt)
   Some try to, but who can?

The self-observed observing Mind
We meet when we observe at all
Is not alarming or unkind
   But utterly banal.

Though instruments at Its command
Make wish and counterwish come true,
It clearly cannot understand
   What It can clearly do.

Since the analogies are rot
Our senses based belief upon,
We have no means of learning what
　Is really going on,

And must put up with having learned
All proofs or disproofs that we tender
Of His existence are returned
　Unopened to the sender.

Now, did He really break the seal
And rise again? We dare not say;
But conscious unbelievers feel
　Quite sure of Judgment Day.

Meanwhile, a silence on the cross,
As dead as we shall ever be,
Speaks of some total gain or loss,
　And you and I are free

To guess from the insulted face
Just what Apperances He saves
By suffering in a public place
　A death reserved for slaves.

Bucolics

1. WINDS

(For Alexis Leger)

Deep, deep below our violences,
Quite still, lie our First Dad, his watch
   And many little maids,
But the boneless winds that blow
   Round law-court and temple
Recall to Metropolis
   That Pliocene Friday when,
At His holy insufflation
   (Had He picked a teleost
Or an arthropod to inspire,
   Would our death also have come?)
One bubble-brained creature said; —
   'I am loved, therefore I am' —:
And well by now might the lion
   Be lying down with the kid,
Had he stuck to that logic.

Winds make weather; weather
Is what nasty people are
   Nasty about and the nice
Show a common joy in observing:
   When I seek an image
For our Authentic City,
   (Across what brigs of dread,
Down what gloomy galleries,
   Must we stagger or crawl
Before we may cry — O look !?)
   I see old men in hall-ways
Tapping their barometers,
   Or a lawn over which
The first thing after breakfast,
   A paterfamilias
Hurries to inspect his rain-gauge.

Goddess of winds and wisdom,
    When, on some windless day
Of dejection, unable
    To name or to structure,
Your poet with bodily tics,
    Scratching, tapping his teeth,
Tugging the lobe of an ear,
    Unconsciously invokes You,
Show Your good nature, allow
    Rooster or whistling maid
To fetch him Arthur O'Bower;
    Then, if moon-faced Nonsense,
That erudite forger, stalk
    Through the seven kingdoms,
Set Your poplars a-shiver
    To warn Your clerk lest he
Die like an Old Believer
    For some spurious reading:
And in all winds, no matter
    Which of Your twelve he may hear,
Equinox gales at midnight
    Howling through marram grass,
Or a faint susurration
    Of pines on a cloudless
Afternoon in midsummer,
    Let him feel You present,
That every verbal rite
    May be fittingly done,
And done in anamnesis
    Of what is excellent
Yet a visible creature,
    Earth, Sky, a few dear names.

2. WOODS

(For Nicholas Nabakov)

Sylvan meant savage in those primal woods
Piero di Cosimo so loved to draw,
Where nudes, bears, lions, sows with women's heads,
Mounted and murdered and ate each other raw,
Nor thought the lightning-kindled bush to tame
But, flabbergasted, fled the useful flame.

Reduced to patches, owned by hunting squires,
Of villages with ovens and a stocks,
They whispered still of most unsocial fires,
Though Crown and Mitre warned their silly flocks
The pasture's humdrum rhythms to approve
And to abhor the licence of the grove.

Guilty intention still looks for a hotel
That wants no details and surrenders none;
A wood is that, and throws in charm as well,
And many a semi-innocent, undone,
Has blamed its nightingales who round the deed
Sang with such sweetness of a happy greed.

Those birds, of course, did nothing of the sort,
And, as for sylvan nature, if you take
A snapshot at a picnic, O how short
And lower-ordersy the Gang will look
By those vast lives that never took another
And are not scared of gods, ghosts, or stepmother.

Among these coffins of its by-and-by
The Public can (it cannot on a coast)
Bridle its skirt-and-bargain-chasing eye,
And where should an austere philologist
Relax but in the very world of shade
From which the matter of his field was made.

Old sounds re-educate an ear grown coarse,
As Pan's green father suddenly raps out
A burst of undecipherable Morse,
And cuckoos mock in Welsh, and doves create
In rustic English over all they do
To rear their modern family of two.

Now here, now there, some loosened element,
A fruit in vigour or a dying leaf,
Utters its private idiom for descent,
And late man, listening through his latter grief,
Hears, close or far, the oldest of his joys,
Exactly as it was, the water noise.

A well-kempt forest begs Our Lady's grace;
Someone is not disgusted, or at least
Is laying bets upon the human race
Retaining enough decency to last;
The trees encountered on a country stroll
Reveal a lot about a country's soul.

A small grove massacred to the last ash,
An oak with heart-rot, give away the show:
This great society is going smash;
They cannot fool us with how fast they go,
How much they cost each other and the gods.
A culture is no better than its woods.

3. MOUNTAINS

(For Hedwig Petzold)

I know a retired dentist who only paints mountains,
    But the Masters rarely care
That much, who sketch them in beyond a holy face
    Or a highly dangerous chair;
While a normal eye perceives them as a wall
Between worse and better, like a child, scolded in France,
Who wishes he were crying on the Italian side of the Alps:
    Caesar does not rejoice when high ground
      Makes a darker map,
    Nor does Madam. Why should they? A serious being
      Cries out for a gap.

And it is curious how often in steep places
    You meet someone short who frowns,
A type you catch beheading daisies with a stick:
    Small crooks flourish in big towns,
But perfect monsters — remember Dracula —
Are bred on crags in castles. Those unsmiling parties,
Clumping off at dawn in the gear of their mystery
    For points up, are a bit alarming;
      They have the balance, nerve,
    And habit of the Spiritual, but what God
      Does their Order serve?

A civil man is a citizen. Am I
    To see in the Lake District, then,
Another bourgeois invention like the piano?
    Well, I won't. How can I, when
I wish I stood now on a platform at Penrith,
Zurich, or any junction at which you leave the express
For a local that swerves off soon into a cutting? Soon
    Tunnels begin, red farms disappear,
      Hedges turn to walls,
    Cows become sheep, you smell peat or pinewood, you hear
      Your first waterfalls,

And what looked like a wall turns out to be a world
    With measurements of its own
And a style of gossip. To manage the Flesh,
    When angels of ice and stone
Stand over her day and night who make it so plain
They detest any kind of growth, does not encourage
Euphemisms for the effort: here wayside crucifixes
    Bear witness to a physical outrage,
        And serenades too
Stick to bare fact; 'O my girl has a goitre,
    I've a hole in my shoe!'

Dour. Still, a fine refuge. That boy behind his goats
    Has the round skull of a clan
That fled with bronze before a tougher metal,
    And that quiet old gentleman
With a cheap room at the Black Eagle used to own
Three papers but is not received in Society now:
These farms can always see a panting government coming;
    I'm nordic myself, but even so
        I'd much rather stay
Where the nearest person who could have me hung is
    Some ridges away.

To be sitting in privacy, like a cat
    On the warm roof of a loft,
Where the high-spirited son of some gloomy tarn
    Comes sprinting down through a green croft,
Bright with flowers laid out in exquisite splodges
Like a Chinese poem, while, near enough, a real darling
Is cooking a delicious lunch, would keep me happy for
    What? Five minutes? For an uncatlike
        Creature who has gone wrong,
Five minutes on even the nicest mountain
    Are awfully long.

4. LAKES

(For Isaiah Berlin)

A lake allows an average father, walking slowly,
    To circumvent it in an afternoon,
And any healthy mother to halloo the children
    Back to her bedtime from their games across:
(Anything bigger than that, like Michigan or Baikal,
    Though potable, is an 'estranging sea').

Lake-folk require no fiend to keep them on their toes;
    They leave aggression to ill-bred romantics
Who duel with their shadows over blasted heaths:
    A month in a lacustrine atmosphere
Would find the fluvial rivals waltzing not exchanging
    The rhyming insults of their great-great-uncles.

No wonder Christendom did not get really started
    Till, scarred by torture, white from caves and jails,
Her pensive chiefs converged on the Ascanian Lake
    And by that stork-infested shore invented
The life of Godhead, making catholic the figure
    Of three small fishes in a triangle.

Sly Foreign Ministers should always meet beside one,
    For, whether they walk widdershins or deasil,
The path will yoke their shoulders to one liquid centre
    Like two old donkeys pumping as they plod;
Such physical compassion may not guarantee
    A marriage for their armies, but it helps.

Only a very wicked or conceited man,
    About to sink somewhere in mid-Atlantic,
Could think Poseidon's frown was meant for him in person,
    But it is only human to believe
The little lady of the glacier lake has fallen
    In love with the rare bather whom she drowns.

The drinking water of the city where one panics
    At nothing noticing how real one is
May come from reservoirs whose guards are all too conscious
    Of being followed: Webster's cardinal
Saw in a fish-pool something horrid with a hay-rake;
    I know a Sussex hammer-pond like that.

A haunted lake is sick, though; normally, they doctor
    Our tactile fevers with a visual world
Where beaks are dumb like boughs and faces calm like houses;
    The water-scorpion finds it quite unticklish,
And, if it shudder slightly when caressed by boats,
    It never asks for water or a loan.

Liking one's Nature, as lake-lovers do, benign
    Goes with a wish for savage dogs and man-traps:
One Fall, one dispossession, is enough, I'm sorry;
    Why should I give Lake Eden to the Nation
Just because every mortal Jack and Jill has been
    The genius of some amniotic mere?

It is unlikely I shall ever keep a swan
    Or build a tower on any small tombolo,
But that's not going to stop me wondering what sort
    Of lake I would decide on if I should.
Moraine, pot, oxbow, glint, sink, crater, piedmont, dimple . . .?
    Just reeling off their names is ever so comfy.

5. ISLANDS

(For Giovanni Maresca)

Old saints on millstones float with cats
    To islands out at sea
Whereon no female pelvis can
    Threaten their agape.

Beyond the long arm of the Law,
   Close to a shipping road,
Pirates in their island lairs
   Observe the pirate code.

Obsession with security
   In Sovereigns prevails;
His Highness and The People both
   Pick islands for their jails.

Once, where detected worldlings now
   Do penitential jobs,
Exterminated species played

   Who had not read their Hobbes.
His continental damage done,
   Laid on an island shelf,
Napoleon has five years more
   To talk about himself.

How fascinating is that class
   Whose only member is Me!
Sappho, Tiberius and I
   Hold forth beside the sea.

What is cosier than the shore
   Of a lake turned inside out?
How do all these other people
   Dare to be about?

In democratic nudity
   Their sexes lie; except
By age or weight you could not tell
   The keeping from the kept.

They go, she goes, thou goest, I go
   To a mainland livelihood:
Farmer and fisherman complain
   The other has it good.

6. PLAINS

(For Wendell Johnson)

I can image quite easily ending up
    In a decaying port on a desolate coast,
Cadging drinks from the unwary, a quarrelsome,
    Disreputable old man; I can picture
A second childhood in a valley, scribbling
    Reams of edifying and unreadable verse;
But I cannot see a plain without a shudder;
    'O God, please, please, don't ever make me live there!'

It's horrible to think what peaks come down to,
    That pecking rain and squelching glacier defeat
Tall pomps of stone where goddesses lay sleeping,
    Dreaming of being woken by some chisel's kiss,
That what those blind brutes leave when they are through is
      nothing
    But a mere substance, a clay that meekly takes
The potter's cuff, a gravel that as concrete
    Will unsex any space which it encloses.

And think of growing where all elsewheres are equal!
    So long as there's a hill-ridge somewhere the dreamer
Can place his land of marvels; in poor valleys
    Orphans can head downstream to seek a million:
Here nothing points; to choose between Art and Science
    An embryo genius would have to spin a stick.
What could these farms do if set loose but drift like clouds,
    What goal of unrest is there but the Navy?

Romance? Not in this weather. Ovid's charmer
    Who leads the quadrilles in Arcady, boy-lord
Of hearts who can call their Yes and No their own,
    Would, madcap that he is, soon die of cold or sunstroke:
These lives are in firmer hands; that old grim She
    Who makes the blind dates for the hatless genera
Creates their country matters. (Woe to the child-bed,
    Woe to the strawberries if She's in Her moods!)

And on these attend, greedy as fowl and harsher
    Than any climate, Caesar with all his They.
If a tax-collector disappear in the hills,
    If, now and then, a keeper is shot in the forest,
No thunder follows, but where roads run level,
    How swift to the point of protest strides the Crown.
It hangs, it flogs, it fines, it goes. There is drink.
    There are wives to beat. But Zeus is with the strong,

Born as a rule in some small place (an island,
    Quite often, where a smart lad can spot the bluff
Whence cannon would put the harbour at his mercy),
    Though it is here they chamber with Clio. At this brook
The Christian cross-bow stopped the Heathen scimitar;
    Here is a windmill whence an emperor saw
His right wing crumple; across these cabbage fields
    A pretender's Light Horse made their final charge.

If I were a plainsman I should hate us all,
    From the mechanic rioting for a cheap loaf
To the fastidious palate, hate the painter
    Who steals my wrinkles for his Twelve Apostles,
Hate the priest who cannot even make it shower.
    What could I smile at as I truged behind my harrow
But bloodshot images of rivers howling,
    Marbles in panic, and Don't-Care made to care?

As it is, though, I know them personally
    Only as a landscape common to two nightmares:
Across them, spotted by spiders from afar,
    I have tried to run, knowing there was no hiding and no help;
On them, in brilliant moonlight, I have lost my way
    And stood without a shadow at the dead centre
Of an abominable desolation,
    Like Tarquin ravished by his post-coital sadness.

Which goes to show I've reason to be frightened
    Not of plains, of course, but of me. I should like
— Who wouldn't? — to shoot beautifully and be obeyed,
    (I should also like to own a cave with two exits);
I wish I weren't so silly. Though I can't pretend
    To think these flats poetic, it's as well at times
To be reminded that nothing is lovely,
    Not even in poetry, which is not the case.

7. STREAMS

(For Elizabeth Drew)

Dear water, clear water, playful in all your streams,
as you dash or loiter through life who does not love
        to sit beside you, to hear you and see you,
    pure being, perfect in music and movement?

Air is boastful at times, earth slovenly, fire rude,
but you in your bearing are always immaculate,
        the most well-spoken of all the older
    servants in the household of Mrs. Nature.

Nobody suspects you of mocking him, for you still
use the same vocables you were using the day
        before that unexpected row which
    downed every hod on half-finished Babel,

and still talk to yourself: nowhere are you disliked;
arching your torso, you dive from a basalt sill,
        canter across white chalk, slog forward
    through red marls, the aboriginal pilgrim,

at home in all sections, but for whom we should be
idolaters of a single rock, kept apart
        by our landscapes, excluding as alien
    the tales and diets of all other strata.

How could we love the absent one if you did not keep
coming from a distance, or quite directly assist,
　　　as when past Iseult's tower you floated
　　　the willow pash-notes of wanted Tristram?

And *Homo Ludens*, surely, is your child, who make
fun of our feuds by opposing identical banks,
　　　transferring the loam from Huppim
　　　to Muppim and back each time you crankle.

Growth cannot add to your song: as unchristened brooks
already you whisper to ants what, as Brahma's son,
　　　descending his titanic staircase
　　　into Assam, to Himalayan bears you thunder.

And not even man can spoil you: his company
coarsens roses and dogs but, should he herd you through a sluice
　　　to toil at a turbine, or keep you
　　　leaping in gardens for his amusement,

innocent still is your outcry, water, and there
even, to his soiled heart raging at what it is,
　　　tells of a sort of world, quite other,
　　　altogether different from this one

with its envies and passports, a polis like that
to which, in the name of scholars everywhere,
　　　Gaston Paris pledged his allegiance
　　　as Bismarck's siege-guns came within earshot.

Lately, in that dale of all Yorkshire's the loveliest,
where, off its fell-side helter-skelter, Kisdon Beck
　　　jumps into Swale with a boyish shouting,
　　　sprawled out on grass, I dozed for a second,

and found myself following a croquet tournament
in a calm enclosure, with thrushes popular:
　　　of all the players in that cool valley
　　　the best with the mallet was my darling.

While, on the wolds that begirdled it, wild old men
hunted with spades and hammers, monomaniac each,
     for a megalith or a fossil,
     and bird-watchers crept through mossy beech-woods.

Suddenly, over the lawn we started to run
for, lo, through the trees, in a cream and golden coach
     drawn by two baby locomotives,
     the god of mortal doting approached us,

flanked by his bodyguard, those hairy armigers in green
who laugh at thunderstorms and weep at a blue sky:
     He thanked us for our cheers of homage,
     and promised X and Y a passion undying.

With a wave of his torch he commanded a dance;
so round in a ring we flew, my dear on my right,
     when I awoke. But fortunate seemed that
     day because of my dream and enlightened,

and dearer, water, than ever your voice, as if
glad — though goodness knows why -- to run with the human
          race,
     wishing, I thought, the least of men their
     figures of splendour, their holy places.

Horae Canonicae

('*Immolatus vicerit*')

1. PRIME

Simultaneously, as soundlessly,
  Spontaneously, suddenly
As, at the vaunt of the dawn, the kind
  Gates of the body fly open
To its world beyond, the gates of the mind,
  The horn gate and the ivory gate
Swing to, swing shut, instantaneously
  Quell the nocturnal rummage
Of its rebellious fronde, ill-favoured,
  Ill-natured and second-rate,
Disenfranchised, widowed and orphaned
  By an historical mistake:
Recalled from the shades to be a seeing being,
  From absence to be on display,
Without a name or history I wake
  Between my body and the day.

Holy this moment, wholly in the right,
  As, in complete obedience
To the light's laconic outcry, next
  As a sheet, near as a wall,
Out there as a mountain's poise of stone,
  The world is present, about,
And I know that I am, here, not alone
  But with a world and rejoice
Unvexed, for the will has still to claim
  This adjacent arm as my own,
The memory to name me, resume
  Its routine of praise and blame,
And smiling to me is this instant while
  Still the day is intact, and I
The Adam sinless in our beginning,
  Adam still previous to any act.

I draw breath; that is of course to wish
    No matter what, to be wise,
To be different, to die and the cost,
    No matter how, is Paradise
Lost of course and myself owing a death:
    The eager ridge, the steady sea,
The flat roofs of the fishing village
    Still asleep in its bunny,
Though as fresh and sunny still are not friends
    But things to hand, this ready flesh
No honest equal, but my accomplice now,
    My assassin to be, and my name
Stands for my historical share of care
    For a lying self-made city,
Afraid of our living task, the dying
Which the coming day will ask.

2. TERCE

After shaking paws with his dog
(Whose bark would tell the world that he is always kind),
    The hangman sets off briskly over the heath;
He does not know yet who will be provided
    To do the high works of Justice with:
Gently closing the door of his wife's bedroom
    (Today she has one of her headaches),
With a sigh the judge descends his marble stair;
    He does not know by what sentence
He will apply on earth the Law that rules the stars:
    And the poet, taking a breather
Round his garden before starting his eclogue,
    Does not know whose Truth he will tell.

Sprites of hearth and store-room, godlings
Of professional mysteries, the Big Ones
   Who can annihilate a city
Cannot be bothered with this moment: we are left,
   Each to his secret cult. Now each of us
Prays to an image of his image of himself;
   'Let me get through this coming day
Without a dressing down from a superior,
   Being worsted in a repartee,
Or behaving like an ass in front of the girls;
   Let something exciting happen,
Let me find a lucky coin on a sidewalk.
   Let me hear a new funny story.'

At this hour we all might be anyone:
It is only our victim who is without a wish
   Who knows already (that is what
We can never forgive. If he knows the answers,
   Then why are we here, why is there even dust?),
Knows already that, in fact, our prayers are heard,
   That not one of us will slip up,
That the machinery of our world will function
   Without a hitch, that today, for once,
There will be no squabbling on Mount Olympus,
   No Chthonian mutters of unrest,
But no other miracle, knows that by sundown
   We shall have had a good Friday.

3. SEXT

I

You need not see what someone is doing
to know if it is his vocation,

you have only to watch his eyes:
a cook mixing a sauce, a surgeon

making a primary incision,
a clerk completing a bill of lading,

103

wear the same rapt expression,
forgetting themselves in a function.

How beautiful it is,
that eye-on-the-object look.

To ignore the appetitive goddesses,
to desert the formidable shrines

of Rhea, Aphrodite, Demeter, Diana,
to pray instead to St. Phocas,

St. Barbara, San Saturnino,
or whoever one's patron is,

that one may be worthy of their mystery,
what a prodigious step to have taken.

There should be monuments, there should be odes,
to the nameless heroes who took it first,

to the first flaker of flints
who forgot his dinner,

the first collector of sea-shells
to remain celibate.

Where should we be but for them?
Feral still, un-housetrained, still

wandering through forests without
a consonant to our names,

slaves of Dame Kind, lacking
all notion of a city,

and, at this noon, for this death,
there would be no agents.

You need not hear what orders he is giving
to know if someone has authority,

you have only to watch his mouth:
when a besieging general sees

a city wall breached by his troops,
when a bacteriologist

realizes in a flash what was wrong
with his hypothesis, when,

from a glance at the jury, the prosecutor,
knows the defendant will hang,

their lips and the lines around them
relax, assuming an expression

not of simple pleasure at getting
their own sweet way but of satisfaction

at being right, an incarnation
of *Fortitudo, Justicia, Nous.*

You may not like them much
(Who does?) but we owe them

basilicas, divas,
dictionaries, pastoral verse,

the courtesies of the city:
without these judicial mouths

(which belong for the most part
to very great scoundrels)

how squalid existence would be,
tethered for life to some hut village,

afraid of the local snake
or the local ford demon,

speaking the local patois
of some three hundred words

(think of the family squabbles and the
poison-pens, think of the inbreeding),

and, at this noon, there would be no authority
to command this death.

III

Anywhere you like, somewhere
on broad-chested life-giving Earth,

anywhere between her thirstlands
and undrinkable Ocean,

the crowd stands perfectly still,
its eyes (which seem one) and its mouths

(which seem infinitely many)
expressionless, perfectly blank.

The crowd does not see (what everyone sees)
a boxing match, a train wreck,

a battleship being launched,
does not wonder (as everyone wonders)

who will win, what flag she will fly,
how many will be burned alive,

is never distracted
(as everyone is always distracted)

by a barking dog, a smell of fish,
a mosquito on a bald head:

the crowd sees only one thing
(which only the crowd can see),

an epiphany of that
which does whatever is done.

Whatever god a person believes in,
in whatever way he believes

(no two are exactly alike),
as one of the crowd he believes

and only believes in that
in which there is only one way of believing.

Few people accept each other and most
will never do anything properly,

but the crowd rejects no one, joining the crowd
is the only thing all men can do.

Only because of that can we say
all men are our brothers,

superior, because of that,
to the social exoskeletons: When

have they ever ignored their queens,
for one second stopped work

on their provincial cities, to worship
The Prince of this world like us,

at this noon, on this hill,
in the occasion of this dying?

What we know to be not possible,
   Though time after time foretold
By wild hermits, by shaman and sybil
   Gibbering in their trances,
Or revealed to a child in some chance rhyme
   Like *will* and *kill*, comes to pass
Before we realize it. We are surprised
   At the ease and speed of our deed
And uneasy: It is barely three,
   Mid-afternoon, yet the blood
Of our sacrifice is already
   Dry on the grass; we are not prepared
For silence so sudden and so soon;
   The day is too hot, too bright, too still,
Too ever, the dead remains too nothing.
   What shall we do till nightfall?

The wind has dropped and we have lost our public.
   The faceless many who always
Collect when any world is to be wrecked,
   Blown up, burnt down, cracked open,
Felled, sawn in two, hacked through, torn apart,
   Have all melted away. Not one
Of these who in the shade of walls and trees
   Lie sprawled now, calmly sleeping,
Harmless as sheep, can remember why
   He shouted or what about
So loudly in the sunshine this morning;
   All if challenged would reply
— 'It was a monster with one red eye,
   A crowd that saw him die, not I.' —
The hangman has gone to wash, the soldiers to eat:
   We are left alone with our feat.

The Madonna with the green woodpecker,
　　The Madonna of the fig-tree,
The Madonna beside the yellow dam,
　　Turn their kind faces from us
And our projects under construction,
　　Look only in one direction,
Fix their gaze on our completed work :
　　Pile-driver, concrete-mixer,
Crane and pick-axe wait to be used again,
　　But how can we repeat this?
Outliving our act, we stand where we are,
　　As disregarded as some
Discarded artifact of our own,
　　Like torn gloves, rusted kettles,
Abandoned branch-lines, worn lop-sided
　　Grindstones buried in nettles.

This mutilated flesh, our victim,
　　Explains too nakedly, too well,
The spell of the asparagus garden,
　　The aim of our chalk-pit game ; stamps,
Birds' eggs are not the same, behind the wonder
　　Of tow-paths and sunken lanes,
Behind the rapture on the spiral stair,
　　We shall always now be aware
Of the deed into which they lead, under
　　The mock chase and mock capture,
The racing and tussling and splashing,
　　The panting and the laughter,
Be listening for the cry and stillness
　　To follow after : wherever
The sun shines, brooks run, books are written,
　　There will also be this death.

Soon cool tramontana will stir the leaves,
  The shops will re-open at four,
The empty blue bus in the empty pink square
  Fill up and depart: we have time
To misrepresent, excuse, deny,
  Mythify, use this event
While, under a hotel bed, in prison,
  Down wrong turnings, its meaning
Waits for our lives. Sooner than we would choose
  Bread will melt, water will burn,
And the great quell begin, Abaddon
  Set up his triple gallows
At our seven gates, fat Belial make
  Our wives waltz naked; meanwhile
It would be best to go home, if we have a home,
  In any case good to rest.

That our dreaming wills may seem to escape
  This dead calm, wander instead
On knife edges, on black and white squares,
  Across moss, baize, velvet, boards,
Over cracks and hillocks, in mazes
  Of string and penitent cones,
Down granite ramps and damp passages,
  Through gates that will not relatch
And doors marked *Private*, pursued by Moors
  And watched by latent robbers,
To hostile villages at the heads of fjords,
  To dark chateaux where wind sobs
In the pine-trees and telephones ring,
  Inviting trouble, to a room,
Lit by one weak bulb, where our Double sits
  Writing and does not look up.

That, while we are thus away, our own wronged flesh
    May work undisturbed, restoring
The order we try to destroy, the rhythm
    We spoil out of spite: valves close
And open exactly, glands secrete,
    Vessels contract and expand
At the right moment, essential fluids
    Flow to renew exhausted cells,
Not knowing quite what has happened, but awed
    By death like all the creatures
Now watching this spot, like the hawk looking down
    Without blinking, the smug hens
Passing close by in their pecking order,
    The bug whose view is balked by grass,
Or the deer who shyly from afar
    Peer through chinks in the forest.

5. VESPERS

If the hill overlooking our city has always been known as Adam's Grave, only at dusk can you see the recumbent giant, his head turned to the west, his right arm resting for ever on Eve's haunch,

can you learn, from the way he looks up at the scandalous pair, what a citizen really thinks of his citizenship,

just as now you can hear in a drunkard's caterwaul his rebel sorrows crying for a parental discipline, in lustful eyes perceive a disconsolate soul,

scanning with desperation all passing limbs for some vestige of her faceless angel who in that long ago when wishing was a help mounted her once and vanished:

For Sun and Moon supply their conforming masks, but in this hour of civil twilight all must wear their own faces.

And it is now that our two paths cross.

Both simultaneously recognise his Anti-type: that I am an Arcadian, that he is a Utopian.

He notes, with contempt, my Aquarian belly: I note, with alarm, his Scorpion's mouth.

He would like to see me cleaning latrines: I would like to see him removed to some other planet.

Neither speaks. What experience could we possibly share?

Glancing at a lampshade in a store window, I observe it is too hideous for anyone in their senses to buy: He observes it is too expensive for a peasant to buy.

Passing a slum child with rickets, I look the other way: He looks the other way if he passes a chubby one.

I hope our senators will behave like saints, provided they don't reform me: He ho4es they will behave like *baritoni cattivi*, and, when lights burn late in the Citadel,

I (who have never seen the inside of a police station) am shocked and think, 'Were the city as free as they say, after sundown all her bureaus would be huge black stones.':

He (who has been beaten up several times) is not shocked at all but thinks, 'One fine night our boys will be working up there.'

You can see, then, why, between my Eden and his New Jerusalem, no treaty is negotiable.

In my Eden a person who dislikes Bellini has the good manners not to get born: In his New Jerusalem a person who dislikes work will be very sorry he was born.

In my Eden we have a few beam-engines, saddle-tank loco-motives, overshot waterwheels and other beautiful pieces of obsolete machinery to play with: In his New Jerusalem even chefs will be cucumber-cool machine minders.

In my Eden our only source of political news is gossip: In his New Jerusalem there will be a special daily in simplified spelling for non-verbal types.

In my Eden each observes his compulsive rituals and superstitious tabus but we have no morals: In his New Jerusalem the temples will be empty but all will practise the rational virtues.

One reason for his contempt is that I have only to close my eyes, cross the iron footbridge to the tow-path, take the barge through the short brick tunnel and

there I stand in Eden again, welcomed back by the krum-horns, doppions, sordunes of jolly miners and a bob major from the Cathedral (romanesque) of St. Sophie (*Die Kalte*):

One reason for my alarm is that, when he closes his eyes, he arrives, not in New Jerusalem, but on some august day of outrage when hellikins cavort through ruined drawing-rooms and fish-wives intervene in the Chamber or

some autumn night of delations and noyades, when the un-repentant thieves (including me) are sequestered and those he hates shall hate themselves instead.

So with a passing glance we take the other's posture. Already our steps recede, heading, incorrigible each, towards his kind of meal and evening.

Was it (as it must look to any god of cross-roads) simply a fortuitous intersection of life-paths, loyal to different fibs?

Or also a rendezvous between two accomplices who, in spite of themselves, cannot resist meeting

to remind the other (do both, at bottom, desire truth?) of that half of their secret which he would most like to forget,

forcing us both, for a fraction of a second, to remember our victim (but for him I could forget the blood, but for me he could forget the innocence),

on whose immolation (call him Abel, Remus, whom you will
it is one Sin Offering) arcadias, utopias, our dear old bag of
democracy are alike founded:

For without a cement of blood (it must be human, it must be
innocent) no secular wall will safely stand.

6. COMPLINE

Now, as desire and the things desired
    Cease to require attention,
As, seizing its chance, the body escapes,
    Section by section, to join
Plants in their chaster peace which is more
    To its real taste, now a day is its past,
Its last deed and feeling in, should come
    The instant of recollection
When the whole thing makes sense: it comes, but all
    I recall are doors banging,
Two housewives scolding, an old man gobbling,
    A child's wild look of envy,
Actions, words, that could fit any tale,
    And I fail to see either plot
Or meaning; I cannot remember
    A thing between noon and three.

Nothing is with me now but a sound,
    A heart's rhythm, a sense of stars
Leisurely walking around, and both
    Talk a language of motion
I can measure but not read: maybe
    My heart is confessing her part
In what happened to us from noon till three,
    That constellations indeed
Sing of some hilarity beyond
    All liking and happening,
But, knowing I neither know what they know
    Nor what I ought to know, scorning

All vain fornications of fancy,
     Now let me, blessing them both
For the sweetness of their cassations,
     Accept our separations.

A stride from now will take me into dream,
     Leave me, without a status,
Among its unwashed tribes of wishes
     Who have no dances and no jokes
But a magic cult to propitiate
     What happens from noon till three,
Odd rites which they hide from me — should I chance,
     Say, on youths in an oak-wood
Insulting a white deer, bribes nor threats
     Will get them to blab — and then,
Past untruth is one step to nothing,
     For the end, for me as for cities,
Is total absence: what comes to be
     Must go back into non-being
For the sake of the equity, the rhythm
     Past measure or comprehending.

Can poets (can men in television)
     Be saved? It is not easy
To believe in unknowable justice
     Or pray in the name of a love
Whose name one's forgotten: *libera*
     Me, libera C (dear C)
And all poor s-o-b's who never
     Do anything properly, spare
Us in the youngest day when all are
     Shaken awake, facts are facts,
(And I shall know exactly what happened
     Today between noon and three)
That we, too, may come to the picnic
     With nothing to hide, join the dance
As it moves in perichoresis,
     Turns about the abiding tree.

7. LAUDS

Among the leaves the small birds sing;
The crow of the cock commands awakening:
In solitude, for company.

Bright shines the sun on creatures mortal;
Men of their neighbours become sensible:
In solitude, for company.

The crow of the cock commands awaking;
Already the mass-bell goes dong-ding:
In solitude, for company.

Men of their neighbours become sensible;
God bless the Realm, God bless the People:
In solitude, for company.

Already the mass-bell goes dong-ding;
The dripping mill-wheel is again turning:
In solitude, for company.

God bless the Realm, God bless the People;
God bless this green world temporal:
In solitude, for company.

The dripping mill-wheel is again turning;
Among the leaves the small birds sing:
In solitude, for company.

Thanksgiving For a Habitat

Funes ceciderunt mihi in praeclaris:
etenim hereditas mea praeclara est mihi.
Psalm XVI, 6

1. PROLOGUE:
THE BIRTH OF ARCHITECTURE
(for John Bayley)

From gallery-grave and the hunt of a wren-king
    to Low Mass and trailer camp
is hardly a tick by the carbon clock, but I
    don't count that way nor do you:
already it is millions of heartbeats ago
    back to the Bicycle Age,
before which is no *After* for me to measure,
    just a still prehistoric *Once*
where anything could happen. To you, to me,
    Stonehenge and Chartres Cathedral,
the Acropolis, Blenheim, the Albert Memorial
    are works by the same Old Man
under different names: we know what He did,
    what, even, He thought He thought,
but we don't see why. (To get that, one would have
    to be selfish in His way,
without concrete or grapefruit.) It's our turn now
    to puzzle the unborn. No world
wears as well as it should but, mortal or not,
    a world has still to be built
because of what we can see from our windows,
    that Immortal Commonwealth
which is there regardless: It's in perfect taste
    and it's never boring but
it won't quite do. Among its populations
    are masons and carpenters
who build the most exquisite shelters and safes,

but no architects, any more
than there are heretics or bounders: to take
umbrage at death, to construct
a second nature of tomb and temple, lives
must know the meaning of *If*.

2. THANKSGIVING FOR A HABITAT
(*for Geoffrey Gorer*)

Nobody I know would like to be buried
    with a silver cocktail shaker,
a transistor radio and a strangled
    daily help, or keep his word because

of a great-great-grandmother who got laid
    by a sacred beast. Only a press lord
could have built San Simeon: no unearned income
    can buy us back the gait and gestures

to manage a baroque staircase, or the art
    of believing footmen don't hear
human speech. (In adulterine castles
    our half-strong might hang their jackets

while mending their lethal bicycle chains:
    luckily, there are not enough
crags to go round.) Still, Hetty Pegler's Tump
    is worth a visit, so is Schönbrunn,

to look at someone's idea of the body
    that should have been his, as the flesh
Mum formulated shouldn't: that whatever
    he does or feels in the mood for,

stocktaking, horseplay, worship, making love,
    he stays the same shape, disgraces
a Royal I. To be overadmired is not
    good enough: although a fine figure

is rare in either sex, others like it
   have existed before. One may
be a Proustian snob or a sound Jacksonian
   democrat, but which of us wants

to be touched inadvertently, even
   by his beloved? We know all about graphs
and Darwin, enormous rooms no longer
   superhumanize, but earnest

city planners are mistaken: a pen
   for a rational animal
is no fitting habitat for Adam's
   sovereign clone. I, a transplant

from overseas, at last am dominant
   over three acres and a blooming
conurbation of country lives, few of whom
   I shall ever meet, and with fewer

converse. Linnaeus recoiled from the Amphibia
   as a naked gruesome rabble,
Arachnids give me the shudders, but fools
   who deface their emblem of guilt

are germane to Hitler: the race of spiders
   shall be allowed their webs. I should like
to be to my water-brethren as a spell
   of fine weather: many are stupid,

and some, maybe, are heartless, but who is not
   vulnerable, easy to scare,
and jealous of his privacy? (I am glad
   the blackbird, for instance, cannot

tell If I'm talking English, German or
   just typewriting: that what he utters
I may enjoy as an alien rigmarole.) I ought
   to outlast the limber dragonflies

as the muscle-bound firs are certainly
  going to outlast me: I shall not end
down any esophagus, though I may succumb
  to a filter-passing predator,

shall, anyhow, stop eating, surrender my smidge
  of nitrogen to the World Fund
with a drawn-out *Oh* (unless at the nod
  of some jittery commander

I be translated in a nano-second
  to a c.c. of poisonous nothing
in a giga-death). Should conventional
  blunderbuss war and its routiers

invest my bailiwick, I shall of course
  assume the submissive posture:
but men are not wolves and it probably
  won't help. Territory, status,

and love, sing all the birds, are what matter:
  what I dared not hope or fight for
is, in my fifties, mine, a toft-and-croft
  where I needn't, ever, be at home *to*

those I am not at home *with*, not a cradle,
  a magic Eden without clocks,
and not a windowless grave, but a place
  I may go both in and out of.

3. THE CAVE OF MAKING
(*In Memoriam Louis MacNeice*)

For this and for all enclosures like it the archetype
  is Weland's Stithy, an antre
more private than a bedroom even, for neither lovers nor
  maids are welcome, but without a

bedroom's secrets: from the Olivetti portable,
  the dictionaries (the very
best money can buy), the heaps of paper, it is evident
  what must go on. Devoid of
flowers and family photographs, all is subordinate
  here to a function, designed to
discourage daydreams — hence windows averted from plausible
  videnda but admitting a light one
could mend a watch by — and to sharpen hearing: reached by an
  outside staircase, domestic
noises and odours, the vast background of natural
  life are shut off. Here silence
is turned into objects.

                          I wish, Louis, I could have shown it you
  while you were still in public,
and the house and garden: lover of women and Donegal,
  from your perspective you'd notice
sights I overlook, and in turn take a scholar's interest
  in facts I could tell you (for instance,
four miles to our east, at a wood palisade, Carolingian
  Bavaria stopped, beyond it
unknowable nomads). Friends we became by personal
  choice, but fate had already
made us neighbours. For Grammar we both inherited
  good mongrel barbarian English
which never completely succumbed to the Roman rhetoric
  or the Roman gravity, that nonsense
which stood none. Though neither of our dads, like Horace's,
  wiped his nose on his forearm,
neither was porphyry-born, and our ancestors probably
  were among those plentiful subjects
it cost less money to murder. Born so, both of us
  became self-conscious at a moment
when locomotives were named after knights in Malory,
  Science to schoolboys was known as
Stinks, and the Manor still was politically numinous:
  both watched with mixed feelings
the sack of Silence, the churches empty, the cavalry

go, the Cosmic Model
become German, and any faith if we had it, in immanent
    virtue died. More than ever
life-out-there is goodly, miraculous, lovable,
    but we shan't, not since Stalin and Hitler,
trust ourselves ever again: we know that, subjectively,
    all is possible.
                        To you, though,
ever since, last Fall, you quietly slipped out of Granusion,
    our moist garden, into
the Country of Unconcern, no possibility
    matters. I wish you hadn't
caught that cold, but the dead we miss are easier
    to talk to: with those no longer
tensed by problems one cannot feel shy and, anyway,
    when playing cards or drinking
or pulling faces are out of the question, what else is there
    to do but talk to the voices
of conscience they have become? From now on, as a visitor
    who needn't be met at the station,
your influence is welcome at any hour in my ubity,
    especially here, where titles
from *Poems* to *The Burning Perch* offer proof positive
    of the maker you were, with whom I
once collaborated, once at a weird Symposium
    exchanged winks as a juggins
went on about Alienation.
                        Who would, for preference,
    be a bard in an oral culture,
obliged at drunken feasts to improvise a eulogy
    of some beefy illiterate burner,
giver of rings, or depend for bread on the moods of a
    Baroque Prince, expected,
like his dwarf, to amuse? After all, it's rather a privilege
    amid the affluent traffic
to serve this unpopular art which cannot be turned into
    background noise for study
or hung as a status trophy by rising executives,

cannot be 'done' like Venice

or abridged like Tolstoy, but stubbornly still insists upon
    being read or ignored : our handful

of clients at least can rune. (It's heartless to forget about
    the underdeveloped countries,

but a starving ear is as deaf as a suburban optimist's :
    to stomachs only the Hindu

integers truthfully speak.) Our forerunners might envy us
    our remnant still able to listen :

as Nietzsche said they would, the *plebs* have got steadily
    denser, the *optimates*

quicker still on the uptake. (Today, even Talleyrand
    might seem a naïf : he had so

little to cope with.) I should like to become, if possible,
    a minor atlantic Goethe,

with his passion for weather and stones but without his silliness
    re the Cross : at times a bore, but,

while knowing Speech can at best, a shadow echoing
    the silent light, bear witness

to the Truth it is not, he wished it were, as the Francophile
    gaggle of pure songsters

are too vain to. We're not musicians : to stink of Poetry
    is unbecoming, and never

to be dull shows a lack of taste. Even a limerick
    ought to be something a man of

honour, awaiting death from cancer or a firing squad,
    could read without contempt : (at

that frontier I wouldn't dare speak to anyone
    in either a prophet's bellow

or a diplomat's whisper).

                    Seeing you know our mystery
    from the inside and therefore

how much, in our lonely dens, we need the companionship
    of our good dead, to give us

comfort on dowly days when the self is a nonentity
    dumped on a mound of nothing,

to break the spell of our self-enchantment when lip-smacking
    imps of mawk and hooey

write with us what they will, you won't think me imposing if
    I ask you to stay at my elbow
until cocktail time: dear Shade, for your elegy
    I should have been able to manage
something more like you than this egocentric monologue,
    but accept it for friendship's sake.

4. DOWN THERE
(*for Irving Weiss*)

A cellar underneath the house, though not lived in,
Reminds our warm and windowed quarters upstairs that
Caves water-scooped from limestone were our first dwellings,
A providential shelter when the Great Cold came,
Which woke our feel for somewhere fixed to come back to,
A hole by occupation made to smell human.

Self-walled, we sleep aloft, but still, at safe anchor,
Ride there on caves: lamplit we dine at street level:
But, deep in Mother Earth, beneath her key-cold cloak,
Where light and heat can never spoil what sun ripened,
In barrels, bottles, jars, we mew her kind commons,
Wine, beer, conserves and pickles, good at all seasons.

Encrust with years of clammy grime, the lair, maybe,
Of creepy-crawlies or a ghost, its flagstoned vault
Is not for girls: sometimes, to test their male courage,
A father sends the younger boys to fetch something
For Mother from down there; ashamed to whimper, hearts
    pounding,
They dare the dank steps, re-emerge with proud faces,

The rooms we talk and work in always look injured
When trunks are being packed, and when, without warning,
We drive up in the dark, unlock and switch lights on,
They seem put out: a cellar never takes umbrage;
It takes us as we are, explorers, homebodies,
Who seldom visit others when we don't need them.

5. UP THERE
(for Anne Weiss)

Men would never have come to need an attic.
Keen collectors of glass or Roman coins build
Special cabinets for them, dote on, index
Each new specimen: only women cling to
Items out of their past they have no use for,
Can't name now what they couldn't bear to part with.

Up there, under the eaves, in bulging boxes,
Hats, veils, ribbons, galoshes, programmes, letters
Wait unworshipped (a starving spider spins for
The occasional fly): no clock recalls it
Once an hour to the household it's a part of,
No Saint's Day is devoted to its function.

All it knows of a changing world it has to
Guess from children, who conjure in its plenum,
Now an eyrie for two excited sisters,
Where, when Mother is bad, her rage can't reach them,
Now a schooner on which a lonely only
Boy sails north or approaches coral islands.

6. THE GEOGRAPHY OF THE HOUSE
(for Christopher Isherwood)

Seated after breakfast
In this white-tiled cabin
Arabs call *the House where
Everybody goes*,
Even melancholics
Raise a cheer to Mrs.
Nature for the primal
Pleasures she bestows.

Sex is but a dream to
Seventy-and-over,
But a joy proposed un-
    -til we start to shave:
Mouth-delight depends on
Virtue in the cook, but
This She guarantees from
Cradle unto grave.

Lifted off the potty,
Infants from their mothers
Hear their first impartial
Words of worldly praise:
Hence, to start the morning
With a satisfactory
Dump is a good omen
All our adult days.

Revelation came to
Luther in a privy
(Crosswords have been solved there):
Rodin was no fool
When he cast his Thinker,
Cogitating deeply,
Crouched in the position
Of a man at stool.

All the Arts derive from
This ur-act of making,
Private to the artist:
Makers' lives are spent
Striving in their chosen
Medium to produce a
De-narcissus-ized en-
    -during excrement.

Freud did not invent the
Constipated miser:
Banks have letter boxes
Built in their façade,
Marked *For Night Deposits*,
Stocks are firm or liquid,
Currencies of nations
Either soft or hard.

Global Mother, keep our
Bowels of compassion
Open through our lifetime,
Purge our minds as well:
Grant us a kind ending,
Not a second childhood,
Petulant, weak-sphinctered,
In a cheap hotel.

Keep us in our station:
When we get pound-noteish,
When we seem about to
Take up Higher Thought,
Send us some deflating
Image like the pained ex-
   -pression on a Major
Prophet taken short.

(Orthodoxy ought to
Bless our modern plumbing:
Swift and St Augustine
Lived in centuries,
When a stench of sewage
Ever in the nostrils
Made a strong debating
Point for Manichees.)

Mind and Body run on
Different timetables:
Not until our morning
Visit here can we
Leave the dead concerns of
Yesterday behind us,
Face with all our courage
What is now to be.

7. ENCOMIUM BALNEI
(*for Neil Little*)

it is odd that the English
                       a rather dirty people
     should have invented the slogan
Cleanliness is next to Godliness
                           meaning by that
     a gentleman smells faintly of tar
persuaded themselves that constant cold hydropathy
     would make the sons of gentlemen
pure in heart
               (not that papa or his chilblained offspring can
    hope to be gentry)
                       still John Bull's
hip-bath it was
               that made one carnal pleasure lawful
     for the first time since we quarrelled
over Faith and Works
              (Shakespeare probably stank
                          Le Grand
    Monarque certainly did)
                   thanks to him
shrines where a subarctic fire-cult could meet and marry
     a river-cult from torrid Greece
rose again
           resweetened the hirsute West
                      a Roman though

bath addict
                    amphitheatre fan
would be puzzled
                         seeing the caracallen acreage
        compressed into such few square feet
mistake them for hideouts
                              warrens of some outlawed sect
        who mortify their flesh with strange
implements
              he is not that wrong
                              if the tepidarium's
        barrel vaulting has migrated
to churches and railroad stations
                              if we no longer
        go there to wrestle or gossip
or make love
                    (you cannot purchase a conjugal tub)
        St Anthony and his wild brethren
(for them ablutions were tabu

                         a habit of that doomed
        behavioral sink this world)
                              have been
just as he thought
                    at work
                         we are no more chaste

                                   obedient
nor
        if we can possibly help it
poor than he was but
                              enthusiasts who were have taught us
        (besides showing lovers of nature
how to carry binoculars instead of a gun)
        the unclassical wonder of being
all by oneself
                    though our dwellings may still have a master
        who owns the front-door key
                              a bathroom

has only an inside lock

                    belongs today to whoever

   is taking a bath

               among us

to withdraw from the tribe at will

                       be neither Parent

   Spouse nor Guest

             is a sacrosanct

political right

          where else shall the Average Ego

   finds its peace

            not in sleep surely

the several worlds we invent as quite as pugnacious

     as the one into which we are born

and even more public

               an Oxford Street or Broadway

   I may escape notice

            but never

on roads I dream of

            what Eden is there for the lapsed

   but hot water

         snug in its caul

widows

      orphans

            exiles may feel as self-important

   as an only child

          and a sage

be silly without shame

              present a Lieder Abend

   to a captive audience of his toes

retreat from rhyme and reason into some mallarmesque

   syllabic fog

         for half an hour

it is wise to forget the time

           our daily peril

  and each other

        good for the soul

once in the twenty-four hour cycle of her body

whether according to our schedule
as we sit down to breakfast
                          or stand up to welcome
    folk for dinner
                to feel as if
the Pilgrim's Way
                or as some choose to call it
                                  the War Path
    were now a square in the Holy City
that what was wrong has been put right
                          as if Von Hügel's
    hoggers and lumpers were extinct
thinking the same as thanking
                          all military hardware
    already slighted and submerged

8. GRUB FIRST, THEN ETHICS (BRECHT)
(*for Margaret Gardiner*)

Should the shade of Plato
    visit us, anxious to know
how *anthropos* is, we could say to him: 'Well,
    we can read to ourselves, our use
of holy numbers would shock you, and a poet
    may lament — "where is Telford
whose bridged canals are still a Shropshire glory,
    where Muir who on a Douglas spruce
rode out a storm and called an earthquake noble,
    where Mr Vynyian Board,
thanks to whose lifelong fuss the hunted whale now suffers
    a quicker death?" — without being
called an idiot, though none of them bore arms or
    made a public splash,' then 'Look!'
we would point, for a dig at Athens, 'Here
    is the place where we cook.'

Though built in Lower Austria,
    do-it-yourself America
  prophetically blueprinted this
    palace kitchens for kingdoms
where royalty would be incognito, for an age when
    Courtesy might think: 'From your voice
and the back of your neck I know we shall get on
    but cannot tell from your thumbs
who is to give the orders.' The right note is harder
    to hear than in the Age of Poise
when She talked shamelessly to her maid and sang
    noble lies with Him, but struck
it can be still in New Cnossos where if I am
    banned by a shrug it is my fault,
  not Father's, as it is my taste whom
    I put below the salt.

    The prehsitoric hearthstone,
      round as a birthday-button
  and sacred to Granny, is as old
    stuff as the bowel-loosening
nasal war cry, but this all-electric room
    where ghosts would feel uneasy,
a witch at a loss, is numinous and again
    the centre of a dwelling
not, as lately it was, an abhorrent dungeon
    where the warm unlaundered meiny
belched their comic prose and from a dream of which
    chaste Milady awoke blushing.
House-proud, deploring labour, extolling work,
    these engines politely insist
  that banausics can be liberals,
    a cook a pure artist

who moves everyman
at a deeper level than
Mozart, for the subject of the verb
to-hunger is never a name:
dear Adam and Eve had different bottoms,
but the neotene who marches
upright and can subtract reveals a belly
like a serpent's with the same
vulnerable look. Jew, Gentile or pigmy,
he must get his calories
before he can consider her profile or
his own, attack you or play chess,
and take what there is however hard to get down:
then surely those in whose creed
God is edible may call a fine
omelette a Christian deed.

The sin of Gluttony
is ranked among the Deadly
Seven, but in murder mysteries
one can be sure the gourmet
didn't do it: children, brave warriors out of a job,
can weigh pounds more than they should
and one can dislike having to kiss them yet,
compared with the thin-lipped, they
are seldom detestable. Some waiter grieves
for the worst dead bore to be a good
trencherman, and no wonder chefs mature into
choleric types, doomed to observe
Beauty peck at a master-dish, their one reward
to behold the mutually hostile
mouth and eyes of a sinner married
at the first bite by a smile.

The houses of our City
    are real enough but they lie
haphazardly scattered over the earth,
    and her vagabond forum
is any space where two of us happen to meet
    who can spot a citizen
without papers. So, too, can her foes. Where the
    power lies remains to be seen,
the force, though, is clearly with them : perhaps only
    by falling can She become
Her own vision, but we have sworn under four eyes
    to keep Her up — all we ask for,
should the night come when comets blaze and meres break,
    is a good dinner, that we
may march in high fettle, left foot first,
    to hold her Thermopylae.

9. FOR FRIENDS ONLY
(for John and Teckla Clark)

Ours yet not ours, being set apart
As a shrine to friendship,
Empty and silent most of the year,
This room awaits from you
What you alone, as visitor, can bring,
A weekend of personal life.

In a house backed by orderly woods,
Facing a tractored sugar-beet country,
Your working hosts engaged to their stint,
Your are unlike to encounter
Dragons or romance : were drama a craving,
You would not have come.

Books we do have for almost any
Literate mood, and notepaper, envelopes,
For a writing one (to 'borrow' stamps
Is a mark of ill-breeding):
Between lunch and tea, perhaps a drive;
After dinner, music or gossip.

Should you have troubles (pets will die,
Lovers are always behaving badly)
And confession helps, we will hear it,
Examine and give our counsel:
If to mention them hurts too much,
We shall not be nosey.

Easy at first, the language of friendship
Is, as we soon discover,
Very difficult to speak well, a tongue
With no cognates, no resemblance
To the galimatias of nursery and bedroom,
Court rhyme or shepherd's prose,

And, unless often spoken, soon goes rusty.
Distance and duties divide us,
But absence will not seem an evil
If it make our re-meeting
A real occasion. Come when you can:
Your room will be ready.

In Tum-Tum's reign a tin of biscuits
On the bedside table provided
For nocturnal munching. Now weapons have changed,
And the fashion in appetites:
There, for sunbathers who count their calories,
A bottle of mineral water.

Felicissima notte! May you fall at once
Into a cordial dream, assured
That whoever slept in this bed before
Was also someone we like,
That within the circle of our affection
Also you have no double.

10. TONIGHT AT SEVEN-THIRTY
(*for M. F. K. Fisher*)

The life of plants
is one continuous solitary meal,
        and ruminants
hardly interrupt theirs to sleep or to mate, but most
        predators feel
ravenous most of the time and competitive
always, bolting such morsels as they can contrive
to snatch from the more terrified: pack-hunters do
        dine *en famille*, it is true,
with protocol and placement, but none of them play host
    to a stranger whom they help first. Only man,
        supererogatory beast,
    Dame Kind's thoroughbred lunatic, can
        do the honours of a feast,

        and was doing so
    before the last Glaciation when he offered
        mammoth-marrow
and, perhaps, Long Pig, will continue till Doomsday
        when at God's board
the saints chew pickled Leviathan. In this age farms
are no longer crenellated, only cops port arms,
but the Law of the Hearth is unchanged: a brawler may not
        be put to death on the spot,
but he is asked to quit the sacral dining area
    instanter, and a foul-mouth gets the cold
        shoulder. The right of a guest
    to standing and foster is as old
        as the ban on incest.

For authentic
comity the gathering should be small
and unpublic:
at mass banquets where flosculent speeches are made
in some hired hall
we think of ourselves or nothing, Christ's cenacle
seated a baker's dozen, King Arthur's rundle
the same, but today, when one's host may well be his own
chef, servitor and scullion,
when the cost of space can double in a decade,
even that holy Zodiac number is
too large a frequency for us:
in fact, six lenient semble sieges,
none of them perilous,

is now a Perfect
social Number. But a dinner party,
however select,
is a worldly rite that nicknames or endearments
or family
diminutives would profane: two doters who wish
to tiddle and curmurr between the soup and fish
belong in restaurants, all children should be fed
earlier and be safely in bed.
Well-liking, though, is a must: married maltalents
engaged in some covert contrast can spoil
an evening like the glance
of a single failure in the toil
of his bosom grievance.

Not that a god,
immune to grief, would be an ideal guest:
he would be too odd
to talk to and, despite his imposing presence, a bore,
for the funniest
mortals and the kindest are those who are most aware
of the baffle of being, don't kid themselves our care

is consolable, but believe a laugh is less
    heartless than tears, that a hostess
prefers it. Brains evolved after bowels, therefore,
    great assets as fine raiment and good looks
        can be on festive occasions,
    they are not essential like artful cooks
        and stalwart digestions.

        I see a table
    at which the youngest and oldest present
        keep the eye grateful
for what Nature's bounty and grace of Spirit can create:
        for the ear's content
one raconteur, one gnostic with amazing shop,
both in a talkative mood but knowing when to stop,
and one wide-travelled worldling to interject now and then
        a sardonic comment, men
and women who enjoy the cloop of corks, appreciate
    depatical fare, yet can see in swallowing
        a sign act of reverence,
    in speech a work of re-presenting
        the true olamic silence.

11. THE CAVE OF NAKEDNESS

(for Louis and Emmie Kronenberger)

Don Juan needs no bed, being far too impatient to undress,
nor do Tristan and Isolda, much too in love to care
    for so mundane a matter, but unmythical
mortals require one, and prefer to take their clothes off,
    if only to sleep. That is why bedroom farces
must be incredible to be funny, why Peeping Toms
    are never praised, like novelists or bird watchers,
for their keenness of observation: where there's a bed,
    be it a nun's restricted cot or an Emperor's
baldachined and nightly-redamselled couch, there are no
    effable data. (Dreams may be repeatable,
but our deeds of errantry in the wilderness of wish

138

so often turn out, when told, to be less romantic
than our day's routine: besides, we cannot describe them
  without faking.) Lovers don't see their embraces
as a viable theme for debate, nor a monk his prayers
  (do they, in fact, remember them?): O's of passion,
interior acts of attention, not being a story
  in which the names don't matter but the way of telling,
with a lawyer's wit or a nobleman's assurance,
  does, need a drawing room of their own. Bed-sitting-rooms
soon drive us crazy, a dormitory even sooner
  turns us to brutes: bone fide architects know
that doors are not emphatic enough, and interpose,
  as a march between two realms, so alien, so disjunct,
the no-man's-land of a stair. The switch from personage,
  with a state number, a first and family name,
to the naked Adam or Eve, and vice versa,
  should not be off-hand or abrupt: a stair retards it
to a solemn procession.
                        Since my infantile entrance
  at my mother's bidding into Edwardian England,
I have suffered the transit over forty thousand times,
  usually, to my chagrin, by myself: about
blended flesh, those midnight colloquia of Derbies and Joans,
  I know nothing therefore, about certain occult
antipathies perhaps too much. Some perks belong, though
  to all unwilling celibates: our rooms are seldom
battlefields, we enjoy the pleasure of reading in bed
  (as we grow older, it's true, we may find it prudent
to get nodding drunk first), we retain the right to choose
  our sacred image. (That I often start with sundry
splendours at sundry times greened after, but always end
  aware of one, the same one, may be of no importance,
but I hope it is.) Ordinary human unhappiness
  is life in its natural colour, to cavil
putting on airs: at day-wester to think of nothing
  benign to memorize is as rare as feeling
no personal blemish, and Age, despite its damage,
  is well-off. When they look in their bedroom mirrors,

Fifty-plus may be bored, but Seventeen is faced by
    a frowning failure, with no money, no mistress,
no manner of his own, who never got to Italy
    nor met a great one: to say a few words at banquets,
to attend a cocktail-party in honour of N or M,
    can be severe, but Junior has daily to cope
with ghastly family meals, with dear Papa and Mama
    being odd in the wrong way. (It annoys him to speak,
and it hurts him not to.)
                                When I disband from the world,
    and entrust my future to the Gospel Makers,
I need not fear (not in neutral Austria) being called for
    in the waist of the night by deaf agents, never
to be heard of on earth again: the assaults I would be spared
    are none of them princely — fire, nightmare, insomnia's
Vision of Hell, when Nature's wholesome genial fabric
    lies utterly discussed and from a sullen vague
wafts a contagious stench, her adamant minerals
    all corrupt, each life a worthless iteration
of the general loathing (to know that, probably,
    its cause is chemical can degrade the panic,
not stint it). As a rule, with pills to help them, the Holy Four
    exempt my nights from nuisance, and even wake me
when I would be woken, when, audible here and there
    in the half-dark, members of an avian orchestra
are already softly noodling, limbering up for
    an overture at sunrise, their effort to express
in the old convention they inherit that joy in beginning
    for which our species was created, and declare it
good.

    We may not be obliged — though it is mannerly — to bless
        the Trinity that we are corporal contraptions,
but only a villain will omit to thank Our Lady or
    her henwife, Dame Kind, as he, she, or both ensemble
emerge from a private cavity to be reborn,
    reneighboured in the Country of Consideration.

12. THE COMMON LIFE

(for Chester Kallman)

A living room the catholic area you
    (Thou, rather) and I may enter
without knocking, leave without a bow, confronts
    each visitor with a style,

a secular faith : he compares its dogmas
    with his, and decides whether
he would like to see more of us. (Spotless rooms
    where nothing's left lying about

chill me, so do cups used for ashtrays or smeared
    with lipstick : the homes I warm to,
though seldom wealthy, always convey a feeling
    of bills being promptly settled

with checks that don't bounce.) There's no *We* at an instant,
    only *Thou* and *I*, two regions
of protestant being which nowhere overlap :
    A room is too small, therefore,

if its occupants cannot forget at will
    that they are not alone, too big
if it gives them any excuse in a quarrel
    for raising their voices. What,

quizzing ours, would Sherlock Holmes infer? Plainly,
    ours is a sitting culture
in a generation which prefers comfort
    (or is forced to prefer it)

to command, would rather incline its buttocks
    on a well-upholstered chair
than the burly back of a slave : a quick glance
    at book titles would tell him

that we belong to the clerisy and spend much
   on our food. But could he read
what our prayers and jokes are about, what creatures
   frighten us most, or what names

head our roll call of persons we would least like
   to go to bed with? What draws
singular lives together in the first place,
   loneliness, lust, ambition,

or mere convenience, is obvious, why they drop
   or murder one another
clear enough: how they create, though, a common world
   between them, like Bombelli's

impossible yet useful numbers, no one
   has yet explained. Still, they do
manage to forgive impossible behaviour,
   to endure by some miracle

conversational tics and larval habits
   without wincing (were you to die,
I should miss yours). It's a wonder that neither
   has been butchered by accident,

or, as lots have, silently vanished into
   History's criminal noise
unmourned for, but that, after twenty-four years,
   we should sit here in Austria

as cater-cousins, under the glassy look
   of a Naples Bambino,
the portrayed regards of Strauss and Stravinsky,
   doing British crossword puzzles,

is very odd indeed. I'm glad the builder gave
   our common-room small windows
through which no observed outsider can observe us:
   every home should be a fortress,

equipped with all the very latest engines
    for keeping Nature at bay,
versed in all ancient magic, the arts of quelling
    the Dark Lord and his hungry

animivorous chimeras. (Any brute
    can buy a machine in a shop,
but the sacred spells are secret to the kind,
    and if power is what we wish

they won't work.) *The ogre will come in any case:*
    so Joyce has warned us. Howbeit,
fasting or feasting, we both know this: without
    the Spirit we die, but life

without the Letter is in the worst of taste,
    and always, though truth and love
can never really differ, when they seem to,
    the subaltern should be truth.

Index of Titles